To my dear friend Susa
Christmas 1996
Love, Sheree

Timeless Treasures

The Charm and Romance
of Treasured Memories

NARRATIVE BY

Emilie Barnes

WITH

Anne Christian Buchanan

PAINTINGS BY

Sandy Lynam Clough

HARVEST HOUSE PUBLISHERS
Eugene, Oregon 97402

Scripture quotations are taken from the King James Version of the Bible.

All works of art reproduced in this book are copyrighted by
Sandy Lynam Clough and may not be copied or reproduced
without the artist's permission. For information regarding art
prints featured in this book, please contact:

Sandy Clough Studios
25 Trail Road
Marietta, GA 30064

OTHER BOOKS BY EMILIE BARNES

*If Teacups Could Talk, Time Began in a Garden, Fill My Cup, Lord,
The Spirit of Loveliness, Prayers and Remembrances,
15 Minutes Alone with God, The Creative Home Organizer,
More Hours in My Day, 15-Minute Family Traditions and Memories,
Survival for Busy Women, Things Happen When Women Care*

*To obtain additional information about Emilie Barnes' seminars and tapes
send a self-addressed, stamped business envelope to:*

MORE HOURS IN MY DAY
2838 Rumsey Drive
Riverside, CA 92506

Art direction, design, and production by
Garborg Design Works, Minneapolis, Minnesota

TIMELESS TREASURES

Copyright © 1996 by Harvest House Publishers
Eugene, Oregon 97402

Library of Congress Cataloging-in-Publication Data

Barnes, Emilie.
    Timeless treasures : the charm and romance of cherished memories / Emilie Barnes
      with Anne Christian Buchanan: paintings by Sandy Lynam Clough
      p.   cm.
    ISBN 1-56507-428-9 (alk. paper)
    1. Antiques—Psychological aspects. 2. Personal paraphernalia-Psychological aspects.
      I. Buchanan, Anne Christian. II. Title.
    NK1125.B356   1995
    745.1—dc20   96-13201
                                                               CIP

Printed in the United States of America.
96 97 98 99 00 01 02 03 04 05 / QH / 10 9 8 7 6 5 4 3 2 1

To all the men and women across the country who shared your hearts and your treasures with me.

Your stories have touched and inspired me.

I wish you many more happy memories.

CONTENTS

Where Your Treasure Is

This is a book about true treasure—about the things we hold in our hands and the memories we hold in our hearts. It's also about the stories that make up our lives.

Again and again, when I was preparing this book, I asked friends and acquaintances to tell me about their timeless treasures—the objects in their lives that hold special meaning for them.

Their eyes would light up and then they would tell me a story. . . .

These men and women entrusted me with precious tales about where they came from, about the people they loved and the people who loved them. They shared stories about how they live and about the objects they choose to surround their lives. They dreamed aloud of treasures they wanted to pass on to their children.

I asked the woman who cleans my house, and I was treated to a beautiful story about a loving grandmother, an inherited Bible, and a mysterious, closed-up room.

I asked the nurses at my doctor's office, and I learned about their collections and their antique furniture. I also learned that one nurse is an only child, that another has a weakness for teddy bears, that yet another received a miniature hope chest for high-school graduation.

I passed out questionnaires in seminars, and I received a shower of touching and delightful stories about antique beds, family cowbells, and buttered noses—plus a recipe or two!

As I listened, I discovered anew the truth of what a Man from Galilee said long ago: Our hearts will be found in the near vicinity of our treasures.

And so this is a book about treasure.

But that also means it is a book about where the heart is.

It is about the special objects in our lives that speak to us about love and hope and memory. It is about preserving yesterday and passing it on to tomorrow in the form of the objects we can see and hear and smell and touch.

The poet Ezra Pound said it so well: "What thou lovest well is thy true heritage."

And that is true of any of us.

Our timeless treasures symbolize what we value most in our lives: love, joy, beauty, hope, family. A delicate cut-glass vase, a brawny set of antique tools, a child's drawing, a grandfather's memoir—any of these can be a timeless treasure if it brings to mind your most beloved relationships, your dearest memories, if it inspires you to reach out and share your story.

Long before you finish this book, I hope you will be digging through your storage boxes, flipping through your photo albums, picking up items one by one and telling their stories to your children. I hope you will be dusting off your pen or your computer, pulling out that half-forgotten scrapbook, working once more on that box of old hankies you hoped (someday) to turn into a baby quilt or those bits of yarn once destined to be an afghan for your sister.

Your timeless treasures represent your true heritage of love and memory. They tell your story—a story that is worth telling.

Keep them close to your heart
And then pass them on.

—*Emilie Barnes*

Inheritance is priceless. Heritage is a treasure.
Clear tracks left behind are the pathway for tomorrow.

— STU WEBER

A Homegrown Heritage

THE STORY YOUR TREASURES TELL

IT'S JUST A BUTTON. A child's button.

White. Heart-shaped. No bigger than my thumbnail, it nestles in my hand.

Not even an antique, it boasts no monetary value.

And yet that button is a timeless treasure to me—because it came from my green gingham dress.

My mother was a dressmaker, a tailor's daughter. Her stitches and her designs and her good taste in clothes were part of her gift to the world, along with her gentle, loving spirit. And the dress she made for me when I was six was a special gift of love.

I remember watching her make it—her skilled feet setting up an intoxicating rhythm as she pumped the old treadle sewing machine. I remember trying it on, watching her finish the seams by hand, and turning up the generous hem for plenty of room to grow. When everything else was finished, she attached the dainty heart-shaped buttons. And then my beautiful dress was ready to wear.

I put it on. The crisp fabric felt rustly and cool. The short sleeves puffed out prettily. The full, gathered skirt swirled just right over my petticoats. I put my hands in the big pockets. I twirled again. I felt like a princess. And I wanted to wear that dress all the time.

At first, though, the green gingham dress was only for special occasions. I wore it to a wedding. To a funeral. And for company. One reason I loved to have my aunts and uncles visit was that I got to wear my special dress.

It was one of those visits, though, that demoted my green gingham to second-best. Our guests were late to arrive that day. I grew tired of waiting and went out to play, only to slip and fall into a nice pile of—well, suffice it to say that a dog had been playing there as well. My beautiful dress was filthy and rather fragrant. Devastated, I pulled myself to my feet and ran crying to my mother.

Mama always knew what to do to comfort me, to make things all right. Very gently, she pulled my special dress off over my head, washed me and the dress, and assured me that my treasure would be fine.

It was, and it wasn't.

The dirt came off, but the dress was no longer new. By the time I started school that fall, the green gingham had become a school dress. Mama made me a new best dress out of the same pattern, but it wasn't the same. I still loved the green gingham, and I wore it whenever I could.

My legs grew longer, and the green gingham dress grew shorter. Mama let out the hem and sewed on a band of white rickrack so the hemline wouldn't show. Soon there were two rows of rickrack, and then three, and finally Mama said I couldn't wear my favorite dress to school anymore. But it would make a fine play dress, she said, with slacks underneath. So I wore it on Saturdays to ride my bike down to the beach.

And then came the day when I just couldn't squeeze into that special dress any longer. I was eight years old—a big girl now. And my beautiful green gingham went into mother's rag box.

By now, though, my mother was teaching me to sew. One of my first projects was to make an apron. Out came the green gingham dress from its rag-box obscurity. We cut off the gathered skirt, added a waistband, made use of the ties and the pockets, and presto, my old friend had become an apron. With leftover fabric Mama and I made a pair of potholders. And the little heart-shaped buttons were snipped off and returned to Mama's button box.

I wore my apron proudly as Mama taught me how to cook and clean. The pockets were big and handy to put in tidbits of trash as I cleaned each little room. The skirt section that had grown too short was just the right size to protect my other clothes. The potholders protected my fingers as I pulled out pans and stirred the food.

But even aprons are outgrown after a time. Eventually my dress-turned-apron grew tattered and stained, and back into the rag box it went. When I saw it next it was torn into pieces. I wish now we'd saved some of them to make a quilt! Instead, the now-soft cotton made fine cloths for dusting and wiping up. One day I saw a big section of my gingham skirt swishing across the floor in a rag mop. (Mama made our mops out of old rags, and they worked beautifully.) The white heart buttons popped up on several subsequent dresses and on a couple of flannel nighties.

> Her plants,
> her books ...
> her writing desk
> ...were all within
> her reach...she
> could scarcely see
> an object in that
> room which had
> not an interesting
> remembrance
> connected with it.
>
> —JANE AUSTEN

Just a Plain Old Rolling Pin

My grandmother was raised in an orphanage until she was thirteen, when she went to work as a household servant. She married my immigrant grandfather, himself a widower and father of one small son, at the age of nineteen. She had little formal education to bring into her marriage, and very little knowledge of healthy family relationships. What she did bring, however, was a merry laugh and a tried-and-true ability to care for a home, prepare delicious and beautiful meals, canning skills, and a gift for baking that is still spoken of by anyone who knew Margaret Sayad.

When my grandfather died, my grandmother moved to my home, bringing all of her worldly possessions with her—and one of these was passed to me. It is a plain, sturdy wooden rolling pin, lacking any particular natural beauty. Yet the worn handles and carved middle are beautiful to me as I remember my grandmother, her kitchen, and all the endless hours she poured into preparing food for those she loves. Every pie I bake brings a brimful of tears to my eyes remembering my dear grandmother and her love for God and others.

When this timeless treasure is passed to my daughter, it will be four generations old.

—Donna Otto, Scottsdale, Arizona

A Room-by-Room Treasure Hunt

Do you know what your treasures are? If your beloved maiden aunt just happened to leave you her three-carat diamond, chances are you would know you own an heirloom treasure. Chances are you would store it away in a safety deposit box or squirrel it away in a Band-aid box (where my mother stored her wedding rings). Sometimes your treasures can be so familiar that you don't recognize them as such. Or sometimes you stash them away and forget you have them. Some treasures may be still at your mother's house or your grandmother's. Some may still be on your "someday" wish list. Just in case your memory needs jogging, here is a list of some of the hidden treasures you may already own:

KITCHEN TREASURES
- recipes
- dishes
- antique utensils
- cabinets
- trays, tea trays
- aprons
- dish towels and tea towels
- decorative tins
- cookie jars

DINING ROOM TREASURES
- sideboards and china
- cabinets
- tables and chairs
- tablecloths and napkins
- china
- tea and coffee service
- napkin rings

PARLOR TREASURES
- furniture
- photo albums, photos
- music and instruments
- knick-knacks
- books
- phonograph albums
- CDs and videos

BEDROOM TREASURES
- quilts
- beds and dressers
- armoires and wardrobes
- dresser sets
- bedspreads and pillowcases
- trunks
- love letters
- sachets
- jewelry (real and costume)

NURSERY TREASURES
- tea sets
- wooden toys
- metal cars and trucks
- books
- games
- dolls
- teddy bears and other stuffed animals

GARDEN TREASURES
- shovels, rakes, plows and other implements
- bulbs and cuttings
- gardening books
- sun hats
- watering cans

LIBRARY TREASURES
- first-edition books
- treasured tomes
- children's books
- personal stories and memoirs
- pictures/paintings

WORKROOM TREASURES
- buttons and boxes
- thimbles
- needle covers
- sewing machines
- knitting needles and crochet hooks
- needlework
- samplers
- antique lace and fabic

WARDROBE TREASURES
- heirloom dresses and lingerie
- christening dresses
- menswear (suits and vests)
- sweaters
- hats and hatpins
- shoes and boots

Two of those little buttons have survived, and one of them is nestled in my hand.

It's just a button, but it is also a memory.

It connects me with my mother, who gave me so much. It reminds me of her gentleness, her understanding, her diligent teaching. When I touch it, somehow I'm touching her as well.

And that button that connects me to my mother also connects me to *me*. It reminds me of the Emilie who was a little girl playing in the yard, a schoolgirl heading off to school, an older girl exploring the beach, a budding homemaker learning to sew and cook and clean.

That one little button tells part of my story.

That's why, for me, it's a timeless treasure.

But it's not my only treasure. In fact, the older I grow, the more I feel I'm surrounded by treasures. The storage boxes in the garage have proliferated, and so have the quilts and spoons and teacups that stack in my corners and adorn my tables and warm my life.

For me, a walk through my house is almost like a visit with a group of old friends. Almost everything I encounter comes with a story attached.

This exquisite, tiny sugar bowl and creamer was a gift from some ladies who approached me at a workshop. They hardly knew me, but somehow they felt I had touched their lives through my speaking and they wanted to give me something in return. Their generosity and thoughtfulness warms my heart whenever I look at their gift.

That elongated wooden bowl is a flea-market find, a prize from one of many treasure-hunting expeditions. When my husband, Bob, and I were first married, we shopped garage sales and thrift shops because that was the only way we could afford to decorate our home. Today we do it mainly for fun, and we still bring home a treasure from time to time!

The quilt in the guest room recalls several visits to an Amish community in Ohio. The simple beauty of the Amish lifestyle struck a chord deep in my soul, and my spirit is calmed when I look at the gentle colors and touch the soft fabrics.

The tangle of silk flowers and vines arranged artfully atop the armoires are a testimony to my daughter Jenny's exuberant spirit and talented hands. The clay pot that holds pencils was sculpted by our son Brad when he was still in high school.

Some of my treasures have monetary value: the English porcelain, a silver bowl from my wealthy auntie, a signed first edition of *The Agony and the Ecstasy* that belonged to my mother. Some are only treasures of my heart: my apron with my grandchildren's handprints, my mama's handbag and hankies, my prayer basket with my Bible and journal and an old hankie.

Some treasures I have gathered deliberately, like my collection of English bone-china teacups and silver teaspoons. Others have eased gradually into my taste, like my auntie's ruby-colored glassware, which I didn't appreciate until I saw it on a table with her china.

And some, perhaps the most precious, were created with the explicit purpose of capturing memories. Each year, for example, we take a family picture and write down memories for our "once a year"

Timeless Treasures

I love them because they are old,
But they never get old to me.
Each one is wrapped in a story
And tied with a memory.

A ragged old album of pictures,
A doll who has lost her hair,
And there's a dress that my grandmother made
And an old pink and blue teddy bear. . . .

These treasures are stored in a trunk
That I barely can stuff them all in.
My grandmother's sewing machine
Holds an old yellow diaper pin.

I wistfully think of the treasures
That I don't even have anymore:
The sweet baby quilt that was lost in a fire,
The clock that crashed to the floor.

Those all were part of my treasures,
And I hated to see them go.
But did losing them give me
great pain in my heart?
Well, actually I have to say "no."

Although they were timeless treasures
That tied me to my past,
They still were only material things
And things can't always last.

It was love that made them heirlooms
And not just antiques you can see.
And it's the unbroken bonds of love
That are real timeless treasures to me.

— SANDY CLOUGH

Christmas album. And each guest in our home autographs our "You Are Special" plate or outlines their hand on the sheet I've used as a special tablecloth. Someday I plan to turn this tablecloth into a one-of-a-kind quilt.

All of these and more are my timeless treasures. They comfort me and they bring me joy. My life is richer when I have them out to see and touch and remember.

And of course they are mine to dust and to wash and occasionally to repair, for maintenance is the price of loving anything on earth, from porcelain to people.

These treasures are mine to pass on—to my children and grandchildren and nieces and nephews and a few special others whom I love. They are my home-grown heritage, and sharing them with those who come after me represents a sharing of hearts and hands across the generations.

More and more, I feel this delightful responsibility is mine.

More and more, I think of myself as a keeper and preserver, a guardian of a treasure trove that belongs to the future.

Will those who come after me want my timeless treasures?

I don't know.

Who can understand the strange alchemy that turns "stuff" into treasure? What lasts and what doesn't is a mystery that challenges even the wisest minds.

What poem, written today, will find itself in tomorrow's textbooks?

What recipe, thrown together in predinner haste, will become a family favorite and be passed down through the generations?

What baby gift, perhaps chosen quickly on the way to a shower, will become a favorite possession and later a treasured memory?

Most likely my descendants will keep some of the treasure I've accumulated in my lifetime. Some they will sell, some they will use, and some they will carefully pack away for even more future generations.

And that is fine with me. I wouldn't want their lives so crowded with my treasures and my stories that they have no room for their own. But I do want to be part of their lives. I want them to be able to touch me, somehow, as they touch the things I have touched.

> *Deep are these roots, inescapable, restorative. I thought about how life had gone on, generation after generation. Perhaps the past is really never gone, but always a part of the present. Lingering there in the quietness, I gathered up the people, the places, the little fragments of another time.*
>
> —HELEN THAMES RALEY

Grandma Had the Blues

When I was young, my grandma had a set of blue-and-white kitchen canisters. I liked to watch her take handfuls and pinches of this and that out of them as she cooked. Oh, the smells and tastes of what came from those blue crocks! She made the best cinnamon rolls!

Perhaps because of those memories, the colors blue and white have always been special to me. As I grew up, I was always drawn to objects made of blue and white. One day,

years later, my father handed me a box. When I opened it and unwrapped the contents, those smells and tastes from long ago immediately filtered through my mind, for my father had given me a most precious gift—a set of original Delft canisters from Germany. They are priceless to me. And now they sit on my kitchen shelves—not just bringing back fond memories, but also filling my family and grandchildren with sweet smells and memories.

—Lynn L. Gramm, Grass Valley, California

I want them to know their heritage and to own something tangible that reminds them of where they came from. So I guard the treasures and I tell the stories.

"This was Grandma Irene's," I tell granddaughter Christine as we fasten the rhinestone brooch on the front of her flowing dress-up dress. "She always loved beautiful clothes and beautiful things."

"This ladle was my daddy's," I tell my friend as we work in the kitchen together. "The chef's knife was his, too. I remember watching him sharpen it on a whetstone. My dad was a wonderful chef, and I've recently discovered he was involved in producing movies, too."

"Why don't you show the children your photo albums?" I urge Bob's mother whenever she babysits for her great-grandchildren. "Tell them about the afghan on your bed. Tell them about your ring. Wasn't it your sister's?"

"And this," I tell the babies, "is a button that came off my very favorite dress when I was a little girl. My mama made it. . . ."

The stories, you see, are the important thing. It is the miracle of memory that transforms a houseful of stuff into a heritage of love and connection.

The treasures I hold closest to my heart, just as that tiny button nestles in my hand, are the ones that are connected to the people I love and the people I have loved. They have meaning because they express something of who I am and where I came from and what I have done.

And your timeless treasures do the same for you.

The true treasures in your life are the ones that are tied to your heartstrings.

Some are beautiful—your great-grandmother's piano or the framed engraving your husband gave you for your birthday.

Some are valuable—an heirloom diamond reset to suit your taste, a first edition of *Ben Hur* or *Gone with the Wind,* your great-great-great grandfather's Civil War diary.

Your treasures may be silly or sad—a terra cotta cat playing a bagpipe or a packet of letters from a love long lost.

Whatever your treasures are, they tell a story about you, about what you love or value or believe in, about what makes you laugh or cry.

Your treasure is your homegrown heritage.

It may be just a button. Or it may be a photo or a watch or a box of recipes.

It's still a heritage worth preserving, worth sharing, worth passing on.

It's still a timeless treasure.

A Treasured Rose

My timeless treasure is a living one—a beautiful Cecile Brunner rosebush.

When my daddy was born in Los Angeles, his family had a Cecile Brunner rose arbor. They kept it blooming until they moved (when his mother died in the 1950s). His father and brother were landscape architects (my grandfather designed most of Beverly Hills, and the rose garden at the Coliseum in Exposition Park, among other things). When I was growing up, Daddy and some of the other older men always wore a single Cecile Brunner rose in their lapels at church on Sundays. When my parents moved to Orange County in 1961, they brought a cutting from the original rosebush in Los Angeles. Now my sister and I each have a Cecile Brunner rosebush in our yards from that bush that grew at my grandmother's Los Angeles home. We wear them on lots of occasions—in addition to decorating presents, making little bouquets around the house, and so on. We've always loved the unique spicy fragrance and delicate blooms as well as the family memories.

—*Carolyn Alex, Santa Ana, California*

I WOULD NEVER SELL IT—BUT....

For insurance purposes (and to satisfy your own curiosity), you might want to find out if your grandma's stickpin or your uncle's pocket watch has any market value. The simplest way to do this is to pay for a professional appraisal. You can get appraisals through auction houses or insurance firms. Some appraisers will be listed in the Yellow Pages under real-estate, and you may be able to get other names through reputable antique stores or museums. Here are some more possible sources of information about the value of your treasures:

*"Antique and Collectibles" price guides. These are the same publications antique dealers use as a guide in setting prices. You can find them in a public library or specialty bookstore.

*Libraries and museums. Curators are usually very helpful if you are respectful of their time. If you have an old flag, contact the Curator of the Division of Textiles of the Smithsonian Institution's Museum of History and Technology. For appraisal of signatures and autographs, try the Library of Congress Division of Manuscripts. Write first and inquire.

*Specialty shops. Take items such as jewelry, watches, coins, and books to shops that sell or repair these items. You can either pay for an appraisal (if they offer that service) or inquire about selling the item. Watch the dealer carefully and try several stores.

*Auction houses. Go on a day when there isn't an auction and ask the auctioneer or appraiser how much you could expect to get for your treasure at an auction should you decide to sell.

*Furniture refinishers. To find out the worth of a piece of furniture, go to a reputable furniture refinisher and ask for estimates on refinishing the piece. The estimate may give you a good sense of how much the piece is worth. Note: Don't have the piece refinished if you suspect it's an antique; refinishing lowers its value.

*Pawnbrokers. These dealers are usually experts on items such as jewelry. They would go broke giving out money on fakes! Take the piece in question to a dealer who has been in business awhile and ask how much he would give you for the piece. Be suspicious if he says it's worthless and still offers to buy it.

Remember that all appraisals are simply estimates of what the item would bring on the current market. There's no way of stating for certain what an object is worth without actually selling it, and then its "worth" is what you can get for it. Even in the mercantile world, the real worth of a timeless treasure is its heritage—its human connections—not its monetary equivalent!

Ringing Memories

A prized possession in our family is a very large cowbell. This bell was found among my grandmother's belongings after her death at the age of 95 in 1986. The bell had been used in her family as she grew up. This bell has a sound like none other—it is loud and piercing. Our son was beginning to participate in competitive athletics at that time, including football. My husband began to ring the bell at his football games—much to the annoyance of the crowd at times. Anytime he didn't ring it, our son would ask about it. This became their signal and communication method for five years of football. Chris would know his dad was there praying for him, loving him, and supporting him.

After high school graduation, my husband had the bell enclosed in a beautiful shadow box along with a precious letter of love, support, and encouragement and a picture of the two of them. Our son says that the bell will come out only when he has a son to love, encourage, and support. Thus from a lowly 100-year-old cowbell a tradition has been born.

—Carrie Barnes, Tulsa, Oklahoma

You can create new heirlooms,
and the memories that make them special,
just by owning them.

—ELAINE MARKOUTSAS

My Favorite Things

THE VERY PERSONAL ART OF COLLECTING

ONE TEACUP IS SIMPLY . . . a teacup.

Two teacups is service for two.

But if you take those two teacups, arrange them on a glass shelf with a lace scarf, and perhaps add a third to keep them company, you have something more than the sum of three teacups.

You have something that can brighten your living space and embellish your memories.

With a teacup or three and an idea for the future, you have a collection—or the beginnings of one.

And a collection doesn't have to be teacups, of course.

In fact, if an object exists on this earth in quantities of more than one, the odds are that someone, somewhere has collected it.

I know a man who collects wooden yardsticks. They hang on nails all around his workshop.

I know another man who collects university T-shirts, acquired on the campuses of schools he visits. He wears his collection on his back, retiring each one when it begins to look worn. His wife has saved all but the most ragged. Someday she wants to make a quilt out of them.

A couple I met in Kansas collect old buggies and sleighs, which they store in a lofty barn. Another friend's extensive bookmark collection nestles in a single shoebox.

Then there are the friends who collect bells and hankies and old books and paperweights and antique gardening tools. We always know what to get them for their birthdays! And what parent doesn't possess a treasured collection of paintings, pots, and pencil holders shaped by small but loving hands?

Whether traditional or offbeat, carefully cataloged or piled in a corner, a collection is as unique as the collector's personality. Yours could begin with an heirloom—your father's stamp collection, your aunt's gathering of glass animals. It may have grown up around an heirloom, or it may just be a grouping of

A Gathering of Angels

Our second child, our beautiful little Emily Louise, died when she was only five months old. Numb with grief, I started looking for some way to honor her and remember her in our home. When someone gave us an angel ornament the first Christmas season after her death, I knew I had found the perfect thing. I bought a miniature tree, set it up on our piano, and hung the little angel upon it. Then I added tiny white lights and decorated the rest of the tree with gold and silver. Three little china angels, a gift from my mother sat at the base. All during that difficult time, that tree offered us a special way to remember our own little angel. The next year we added another angel ornament to our tree, and every year since then we have collected another one. Now the tree is crowded with a collection of lovely little angels.

Our angel tree has been very special to us and a unique way to remember our daughter. Even now, many years after little Emily died, I find that my angel collection helps me address the ongoing pain (for the loss of child is something you never completely get over). I've also found that it helps other people. It tells visitors that it's all right to talk about our little daughter, and it gives people the opportunity to give a gift they know we will love. We're always happy to receive another angel, and we always appreciate the love and care and remembrance it represents.

—*Ellen Cashmer, Riverside, California*

things that you like—anything from autographs to zippers.

No matter what your collection is—a gathering of glass bells on a table, an arrangement of antique fans in a glass case, a parade of miniature elephants lined up on a windowsill—it probably tells an eloquent story of who you are and what you love (and who has loved you).

To borrow a phrase from Oscar Hammerstein, your collection is a gathering of your favorite things. It is something to lift your spirits on a gray day, something to bring you a smile when your eye lights upon it.

A collection is more than a possession; it's also a pastime. Collections require participation, even if it's only a matter of dusting. For most of us, it's also a matter of sorting and displaying, researching, swapping tales with collectors, and, of course, helping the collection grow.

And the best collections come with a history.

That's why "naming" or "telling" the collection is so integral a part of the entire experience. Each piece in a collection has its own individual story to add to the group history:

"Do you see that tiny little horse in the middle? I've had that since I was a little girl; I bought it at Woolworth's with my own money. That brown one was a gift from my husband when we were dating. I bought that one as a souvenir when we were in Kentucky for vacation. And this one. . . ."

Of course, it is possible to adopt a collection full blown. Decorators often put together instant collections for their clients. Young people in their first apartments may quickly assemble a collection of like objects to fill the empty space on a wall or windowsill. Children in a gift shop may

> No matter what item you think of, somewhere in this country there have got to be people collecting it—and they likely have clubs and papers and annual meetings where they get together and swap and talk about their collections. . . . The main thing I'd like to show is that if something interests you, go ahead and start collecting it. It's bound to become more valuable with time.
>
> —MARGUERITE ASHWORTH BRUNNER

A Quilter's Story

A few years back I began quilting as a hobby. Not long afterward, I began my thimble collection. I don't go for the decorative ones; I like the old advertising thimbles that I used to pick up for pennies and are now scarce. I have a few campaign thimbles from the Depression. (I wish they said "Hoover" or "Roosevelt" but I haven't gotten that lucky yet!)

What I like best about my thimbles is the way they are worn. You see, if you quilt with a thimble, you will begin to have a favorite "place" on that thimble where your needle will rest. If you sew with that thimble for years, a little hole will be cut there. At that time, you should discard or repair the thimble; otherwise, the head of the needle will pop through and hurt your finger.

Some of these Depression-era thimbles have not one, but several little holes worn through, which means these ladies must have injured their fingers regularly, but could not afford to replace the thimble. When you see these worn thimbles, the poverty and frugality of those sewers is poignant. I keep the thimbles in an old tin Whitman's Sampler box that was my mom's when she was little.

—Kathy Garriott, Anderson, South Carolina

purchase a prefabricated rock or shell collection—with the specimens already sorted, mounted, and neatly labeled in their little compartments.

But the best collections and the truly timeless treasures are the ones that grow over time, the ones that are shaped by the personality of the collector and by the events in that person's life. As the years go by, these hands-on collections develop the rich patina of memory. What we have chosen to gather together tells even more about who we are than the single treasures we have accumulated. The act of collecting in itself is a way of shaping our reality, of organizing our existence. Who we are shapes the way our collections begin and the way they grow.

I began my own teacup collection quite deliberately, informing friends and relatives I would welcome china teacups as gifts. (In this sense, a bride who "registers" for a set of china or silver begins a very specialized collection.) But many collections begin by accident. Someone gives you a mug with a funny saying on it. Another funny mug arrives on your birthday. You see one in a store that you like, so you bring it home, then someone realizes you like funny mugs and brings you one back from a vacation. Before you know it, your mugs are overflowing your cabinets and begging for a home of their own.

My friend Jody's doll collection began with a pivotal incident in her young life—when her mother decided Jody was too old for dolls and threw away several beloved friends. Heartbroken, Jody pleaded for just one doll, and her sympathetic grandparents bought her a baby doll for her twelfth birthday. That was the beginning of a doll collection that now includes babies, Barbies, a Shirley Temple, an exquisite French porcelain creation. To Jody, her growing doll collection is a conscious statement that she's not too old for what she loves, and that she can be whoever she wants to be.

Collections can accrue naturally from another kind of interest. What cook doesn't amass a collection

Teacups Do Talk

It was early in the morning, much earlier than I liked to be up, and mother's kitchen seemed cold and lonely without her. Mom was lying in the bedroom, just home from the hospital after a serious heart attack. Dad had called at four that morning to say they needed me, and I had rushed over. After doing what I could to get Mom comfortable, I made a run to the all-night pharmacy and the grocery store and then went into the kitchen to prepare some breakfast.

Sleepily, almost mechanically, I walked over to the cabinet to get some dishes. And there, sitting on the top shelf in plain view, was a gorgeous teacup and saucer.

I stared at it in amazement. I had been in that cabinet many times over the years, and never, never had I seen a fine piece of china in mother's belongings. My mother had grown up during the Depression and was very poor. Later, as the mother of eight, she had always put her children's needs before her own. As long as I

could remember, my mother's morning coffee cup had been a plastic thermos top, so the delicate, fragile beauty of this teacup seemed out of place.

I carefully carried the teacup to Mom in the living room to question where it came from and why I hadn't seen it before. She assured me that someone had given it to her years before. "Why don't you wrap it up and take it home?" she told me.

Mom changed her address from earth to heaven just a month after she came home from the hospital. Now her favorite thermos cup sits in my cabinet right beside that special teacup. Both are constant reminders of my mother's humble and beautiful spirit, her unselfishness and generosity. My mom and I never had the opportunity to discuss my new passion for teacups (which is growing into a collection), but God knew this precious gift would always let me feel Mom's love as well as His. "Teacups do talk."

—Deborah Burnside, Florence, Alabama

A Home for Your Collections

First you begin your collection. Then, almost immediately, you are faced with the inevitable: Where can I display it? If you have a collection you love, you want to have it out to enjoy. Here are some ideas.

• *Don't forget the obvious.* Many collections are for use as well as looks. The simplest place to put these collections is out in the open. Hang antique kitchen implements in the kitchen. Stack your treasured books and Bibles on shelves and lamp tables where they can be read and enjoyed. Cluster a group of picture frames on a table. Spread quilts on your beds.

• *Always group your collection* (or parts of your collection) for display. A small crowd of teddy bears in the corner of a room or a parade of glass bottles in a windowsill will be far more appealing and fulfilling to you than lonely individual items stationed around your house. If your collection is large and space is small, consider breaking the large collection into smaller groups or rotating the items on display.

• *Mass small collectibles together to give them more visual weight.* Crowd small toys together on a table or gather your collection of tiny glass jars on a mirror or tray. Type trays from old printing and wooden cola cases have long been popular for displaying miniature collectibles. Use your imagination. Try baskets, muffin tins, jewelry boxes with drawers open.

• *If your collection is a valuable one, it's worth investing in the hardware to display it properly.* Glass-topped coffee tables and display cases can be quite appropriate for a treasured collection. Special hangers for quilts and textiles can be purchased in quilting shops or through ads in quilting magazines.

• *Large textiles such as quilts and lace tablecloths make beautiful wall hangings.* See chapter 6 for details on caring for your fabric treasures.

• *Remodeled armoires or wardrobes can make beautiful, functional display cases.* Or an extra closet, outfitted with shelves and lights, makes an ideal home for a large collection.

• *Short on wall or cabinet space?* Look up, down, and in corners for forgotten opportunities. Could you run a plate rail above a window or around a small room? Could custom-made shelves be tucked under the stairs or along a hallway? Could you group your collection on a bed or floor? One creative woman transformed an unused fireplace into a cozy den for stuffed animals.

• *Old store fixtures (sewing displays, glove racks, and so forth) make unique and interesting collection cases.* Look for these at flea markets and antique stores, or check the want ads for stores that are going out of business.

• *Don't overlook hooks and hangers, especially for textiles and small items.* Hang a collection of antique vests on covered hangers around a room.

• *Quilts and coverlets don't have to be stretched out on a bed or on a wall.* Stack a collection of colorful quilts on a shelf or under a table with the colorful sides showing.

• *A collection of memorabilia from your children can make an eye-catching display.* Try matting a group of your daughter's paintings and hanging them in your office or hallway. Buy a special bookcase to display clay sculptures and Popsicle-stick creations. Arrange baby clothes and favorite toys in a shadowbox for a unique decoration.

• *Be creative.* I know a nine-year-old who solved the question of where to keep her collection of handpainted but outgrown T-shirts. Now every large teddy bear and stuffed rabbit on her bed wears its own T-shirt!

of cookbooks (and perhaps an assortment of fascinating utensils and maybe some antique implements for interest)? I have seen the walls in a musician's house hung with harps, drums, flutes, and dulcimers—all ready to take down and play. In a backpacker's home, I have smiled at a collection of walking sticks arranged like a bouquet in an umbrella holder.

Why are collections so satisfying? I think they must satisfy some inborn instinct to accumulate, to gather together the things that we like, to have more of a good thing. Children, after all, are natural collectors. Ask any mother who has stubbed her toe on a basket of "pretty rocks" or stolen out to the garbage with a box of plastic fast-food "prizes."

But there's more to collecting than just the pleasure of accumulating. Collections also fill our need to organize our lives, to assign meaning to the miscellany of our experience and give our belongings the stamp of our own personality.

A collection, after all, is more than a group of related objects. It is a group of objects chosen for a reason, with a human personality applied to their acquisition, arrangement, and care. By the very act of collecting something, we are assigning it a meaning—just as we assign meaning to the various experiences of our days by "collecting" them in our memories.

That's not to say that all collections must be strictly categorized and controlled! Successful collecting does not require lining up neatly labeled specimens in regimented rows, unless that is important to you.

The size and shape and organization of collections vary with the people who collect them. One collector thrives amid a friendly jumble on cabinets and windowsills; another orders elegant, custom-built shelves and niches or arranges her treasures very precisely under glass.

Whatever the style, each collector imposes some sense of order on her treasures, even if it's only a matter of piling the teddy bears together in one room. And in the process, she will be proving to herself that order and stability and continuity are truly possible in this often-confusing world. Collections are comforting because they are signs that we have made a mark on our own life. Collections attest to stability, to continuity; they connect our past to our present. They say to the world and to ourselves: "I have been here. I put this together."

But comfort and meaning are not the only advantages our collections bring us. Collections can also be sources of comradeship and conversation. No doubt there are collectors who hoard their treasures in a vault and pore over them in secret like the traditional picture of a miser sifting gold coins through his fingers, but those are not the collectors I know. My friends who have collections love to show them off, take visitors on tours, spiel off the stories of their collected treasures. Collecting invites conversation, stimulates storytelling. It also draws others in, to start collections of their own or to add to the collection of a friend. Collecting is contagious!

A collection of pink lusterware teacups gathers on my grandfather's Queen Anne table across from a lineup of remote-control devices for the TV, the VCR, the stereo. Who is to say which collection is more "serious," or more valuable?

—BO NILES

And collections, like other living, growing things, tend to reproduce. You begin with a collection of dolls, and then somehow you acquire a collection of stuffed animals, which may somehow spawn a gathering of antique wooden toys. My own teacup collection, like the airplane plants on my patio, seems to have sent off shoots that sprouted and grew. I began with a teacup collection; now I collect teapots, antique silver spoons, children's tea sets, children's books, and more.

And collections are fun! Why shouldn't they be? There is a thrill in the hunt for new additions. There is enjoyment in the contemplation of a nicely arranged grouping. There is satisfaction in devising a creative new way of showing off beloved old things. There is peace in living among one's well-loved possessions.

Those of us who love collecting are eager to share the experience by starting collections for the people we love.

It was many Christmases ago that I bought a box at my local Pic-N-Save store. It was a padded, heart-shaped container covered with pretty calico. In it, carefully nested in colored tissue, I placed a china teacup and saucer. Then I tied the whole package with a big bow, added a gift tag, and placed it under the Christmas tree for my granddaughter Christine. I was almost more excited than she was when she opened it on Christmas morning. Together we oohed and aahed over the pretty pattern as we held the delicate porcelain up to the light.

"I want you to give the box back to me," I told her as she cradled her cup in her hands, "and I'll fill it again on your birthday."

That was one teacup. But even before the second teacup arrived and then the third, Christine and I knew it was something more. It was a bond between the two of us, and it was the beginning of a collection that could grow as she grows, that she could share with her children and, I hope, pass on to her grandchildren.

One little teacup can hold a lot of treasure.

There is a passion for hunting something deeply
implanted in the human breast.

— CHARLES DICKENS

What's in Granny's Attic?

TREASURE HUNTING FOR FUN AND POSSIBILITIES

WHEN I WAS A CHILD, I LOVED STORIES about boys and girls who climbed into their granny's attic and discovered trunks full of treasure: old books, mothballed curtains and costumes, discarded lamps, retired baby carriages.

What a perfect way to spend a rainy day, I thought, *up there among all that dusty treasure!*

When I grew up and married and began to decorate my first tight-budget apartment, a different kind of granny's-attic story tickled my imagination. I tore out countless magazine articles about how "junk from the attic" could be refurbished and put to new, creative use. I could transform that old, ugly card table set into an adorable dinette. That old jug could have a new life as a quaint lamp. Those stained doilies and bits of lace could adorn a quilt or a pillow. With ideas like those, granny's attic seemed like even more of a treasure trove.

But I had just one difficulty when I wanted to go up into granny's attic: I didn't have an attic. I didn't even have a granny. My father was an orphan. My mother's parents died long before she moved west and married, so I never knew any of my grandparents. And we never had room during my childhood for accumulating dusty attics full of treasure. When I was small, we moved from one small rented house to another. After my father died, we lived in three tiny rooms behind my mother's dress shop. My mother's prized possessions were beautiful—she always had an eye for quality—but they were few. She had long ago perfected the art of keeping what was essential and leaving the rest behind.

So I never got to play in granny's attic on a rainy day.

But that didn't deprive me of a treasure hunt. I simply learned to find my granny's attics away from home.

Whenever I meander through a downtown antiques mall, whenever I visit rummage sales and flea markets and swap meets, I am really running up those attic stairs to see what I can find.

That's why you'll see me rummaging carefully through precarious stacks of china in an out-of-the way shop. That's why you'll see Bob and me combing through high weeds in a junkyard to find just the right piece of farm equipment to hang on the side of our garage. That's why you'll find me peering into the dark corners of a thrift store just to make sure they don't have any "orphan" silver spoons to add to my collection.

I love to try on dainty and elegant hats from another era.

I love to flip the pages of yellowed photo albums and wonder, "Who's this?" to finger fragile pieces of antique lace and wonder, "Who made it?"

I love to unearth a rusty "mystery gadget" and dream of what I could do with just a little soap and water, a little paint, a little elbow grease, and a lot of imagination.

I treasure the time I spend in granny's attic—wherever I find it.

And yes, I have found wonderful treasures there. Some of it even has monetary value—a silver tea service, an oak icebox used to store glassware, a needlepoint stool. But the majority of my granny's-attic treasures are investments only in memories. I am not looking to buy for little and sell for more. I am not looking for a priceless antique someone overlooked.

I am far from an expert in the field of antiques and collectibles. Chances are, if a hidden treasure is obvious enough for me to spot, someone else has spotted it first.

So I don't worry too much about uncovering priceless treasures when I go to granny's attic. I'm in this game for love more than money. I'm in it for the fun and the possibilities. And I find them aplenty in granny's attic.

I do have a few rules, though, that help me decide what I buy. They're not the rules of the antique specialist or the professional collector, but simply guidelines that help me focus and decide what treasures to bring home with me.

First of all, I buy only what I love. An item needs to call to me, to catch my fancy. Something about it needs to say "treasure" or at least "potential treasure." In one way or another, it needs to tell my story.

Second, I buy what I can use. I try not to purchase any potential treasure just because "it's a bargain." Instead,

Grandpa's Special Chair

One of my fondest memories from my childhood is spending time in my Grandpa's lap as he sat in his favorite chair. Living with my father's parents during the early, formative years of life gave me an opportunity to know and love this large, gentle man with the soft voice. It was often that I would climb up into his lap while he held a book in his rough, work-worn carpenter's hands and read to me. Many years later, when I was about to be a grandmother myself, my aunt called to ask if I might be interested in having this "old chair" of my grandfather's before they donated it to a thrift shop. Without a moment's hesitation I told her I had just the spot! Today it proudly sits in our Americana room and is a sweet reminder of my carpenter grandfather.

—*Barbara J. Howe, Grass Valley, California*

Outfitted for Treasure

Adopting treasure can be an adventure, and any adventure goes better with proper equipment. Although conditions vary—an outdoor swap meet or market is very different from an air-conditioned antique shoppe—you will have more fun if you are comfortable. Here, is a checklist based on the advice of many veteran treasure hunters:

• *Comfortable clothes and shoes.* Unless you are browsing in an exclusive antique district, jeans and tennis shoes are recommended.

• *Something to carry your treasures.* A tote bag can help you avoid frequent trips to the car. Or take a hint from frequent flyers and pull a rolling carry-on bag. Boxes, newspaper, and even bubble wrap in the trunk of your car will help ensure that you get everything home safely.

• *Notebook.* Lists of "I want" items and crucial measurements in your home (doorway sizes, ceiling heights, and so on).

• *Tape measure.* This helps you avoid bringing home a desk that won't go through the doorway or a rug that doesn't fit your floor.

• *Pocket knife.* For scraping away paint to see what's underneath. A Swiss Army knife will also give you a screwdriver, handy for unscrewing the backs of pictures to check whether the print is original. Reputable dealers won't mind your taking a closer look as long as you don't damage the merchandise.

• *Magnifying glass.* For reading manufacturer's marks, spotting cracks and repairs, and zeroing in on "Made in Japan" signs.

• *Small magnet.* To help you tell the difference between brass (nonmagnetic) and iron or steel.

• *Toilet paper.* Don't laugh! In large malls and markets, bathroom maintenance can be minimal. One flea-market veteran recommends keeping a roll in the car and carrying enough paper in your pocket for at least two stops.

• *Flashlight.* Handy for poking around in the basement or the attic at house sales.

• *Price guides and books.* Don't carry them in plain sight or shop owners will be likely to charge you the full "book" price or higher.

I ask myself, "What will I do with it?" I don't mean that it has to be merely utilitarian. Sometimes the use will be decorative or sentimental.

Perhaps that little teddy bear will look wistful on the window seat in our "princess" guest room. Perhaps that basket will add texture and beauty hanging from the dining room ceiling with others of its kind. Perhaps it will make a perfect gift for someone I love, like the silver tea service I found for my daughter-in-law, Maria. After scouring shops across the country for months, I discovered the perfect one right in my own town—on a shopping trip to research this book!

An item might be an appropriate addition to one of my collections: another teacup or silver spoon or quilt or miniature tea set. Perhaps I can see a future for it in a different form: That badly stained pillowcase with the lovely embroidery could be cut into lovely little potpourri bags for a wedding or the drawers from that broken chest would make pretty planters.

My third rule is really a variant of the second: I buy what I have room for. I ask, "Where might I put it?" This question is more appropriate than ever in these days when attics are harder and harder to come by and living spaces are growing smaller. A massive Victorian armoire can quickly stifle a tiny bedroom, and even a petite little table can be in the way if the living room is already crammed. Buying for "someday" is pointless if there's no place to store tomorrow's treasures. So even if an item passes the love test and the usefulness test, the "Where do I put it" test can be a lifesaver.

Finally, if an item calls to me and I can think of a use and space for it, I consider price. My budget stretches a little farther these days than it did when I was first married, but I could easily break it without this guideline. I try not to pay more for a granny's-attic item than I would pay for a new item to fill the same function. I would rather pay much less.

These four little rules have served me well in my many years of "attic" shopping. You can find so much that brings you joy and delight if you follow the principle of buying what you like and what interests you because it fits a need for a price that feels reasonable to you.

But there's a fifth rule that is equally as important, perhaps most important: All the rules were made to be broken—except the first one!

There are times when I will pay more for a piece than feels comfortable—if the item is truly unique or special. There are times when I will buy something without a clear idea of how I will use it or where I will put it. But I will not buy an item I dislike just because it's popular or I think it might be valuable someday or because it was just too cheap to pass up.

If this seems obvious, let me assure you it's not. There is something about the atmosphere of an attic that brings on "gotta have it" fever. Sometimes it's hard to go home without buying *something*. But if you hold to the principle that you have to love it before you buy it, you will be able to develop at least a partial immunity.

And there's a corollary to this fifth rule: We are allowed to break any of the rules for the sake of someone we love.

That is how I acquired my first set of Dionne quintuplet spoons.

You see, I am named after two of those little French Canadian girls that caused such a stir in the forties. My older brother named me after them before I was even born.

One day my pregnant mother and three-year-old Edmund were cuddling on the couch, looking at pictures in magazines. "You know," my mother told him gently, "you're going to have a new little brother or sister soon. What do you think we ought to name the baby?"

Immediately Edmund pointed to a picture in the magazine. It showed two of the Dionne quintuplets, Emilie and Marie. So when I was born a few months later, Mother took brother Edmund's suggestion and named me Emilie Marie.

Growing up, I always loved my name (although the only other Emilies I met in those days were old ladies) and the story about how I was named. So you can imagine my delight when Bob and I happened upon an entire set of Dionne quintuplet souvenir spoons in a murky corner of a San Diego antique store. Each of the five little silver spoons had a little girl on the handle, and you could turn her over to see the back of her dress. Each had the name of a quint engraved on it: Annette, Yvonne, Cecile, and yes, Emilie and Marie.

Those spoons were charming and I loved them immediately, but they were quite expensive—much more than I would normally pay for a little silver spoon or a decorative item.

Some of its mane is gone, the paint is chipped, but that's what makes it so wonderful. Don't you just know it was well loved!

—FLAVIA WEEDN

Reluctantly following my own rule, I handed them back to the owner to replace in their case and walked out into the San Diego sunshine.

Bob caught up with me a few steps later. "Why don't we sit down on this bench and catch our breath?" Then he handed me the little packet with the spoons in it. Knowing how intrigued I was over those special spoons, he had sneaked back into the shop and bought them for me.

My Dionne quintuplet spoons now hold a place of honor on a shelf in my china cabinet. I love to show them to people; they tell a story about me just as eloquently as if they had been stored away for me by my mother or grandmother. I hope my children will love them as much as I do, especially because I now have more than one set.

Several years after Bob bought me my spoons, we traveled to Canada to do a seminar. While staying in Edmonton we decided to visit a large antique show, and there I discovered the second set of quint spoons still in their plastic wrapper.

Without hesitation this time, I bought those spoons and stored them away. Someday they may be an appropriate gift for another little girl named Emilie Marie. If so, I will tell her the story of how she got her name and how her special spoons came to be adopted. Together, we will hold the spoons and turn them over and perhaps wonder where they lived before they came to live with me.

That is another great joy that comes from treasure hunting in antique stores and flea markets. I like to think that I am adopting somebody else's memories, extending a heritage that might otherwise be forgotten. I always hope my treasure was well loved, and I like to imagine the person who owned my treasure before I did.

Was she happy?

A Doll Named Tootsie

It was 1931. A little boy named Leon, walking through an alley, discovered a discarded rag doll. He carried her home to his mother, who cleaned up the doll and made new clothes for her. Then the two of them gave the freshened-up doll as a Christmas present to Leon's little two-week-old cousin—my mama. Leon had named the baby "Tootsie" the day she was born, and he gave the same name to this lonely doll in search of a home.

Mama grew up loving her adopted rag doll. All during her Depression-era childhood she played with her, and she kept her during her teenage wartime years. When she grew up and got married in 1951, she took Tootsie with her. She has kept her all these years, and Tootsie has brought joy to our entire family. She has listened to all our hearts and secrets and always was there for each of us when we felt lonely or sad or had a tear.

Years have passed, and Tootsie is now sixty-four-years old but she has hidden her age well and still is as dear as ever. Tootsie holds a place of honor to this day in our family and sits in the entry area of Mama and Dad's home on a special bench that my dad made for her. Mama has left instructions in her will that when she dies the family is not to give Tootsie away! She wants me, as her only daughter, to take Tootsie and let her come live with me to be passed down through the family from generation to generation.

So, if any of you ever find a lonely doll thrown away, remember this story of Tootsie and give a doll a home! You never know what joy you could bring to someone's life or what timeless treasures and memories you might be creating.

—Penny Hollowell, Ontario, California

Happy Hunting Grounds
WHERE TO FIND GRANNY'S ATTIC

Whether or not you have a granny or an attic, you can enjoy the experience of unearthing and adopting forgotten treasure. Here are some likely sources.

• *Garage and yard sales.* Look for signs in your neighborhood as well as notices in the want ads (under garage sales) and in "Thrifty Bargain"-type advertising papers. Bring your kids—they love garage sales.

• *Church and charity rummage sales.* Many of these are annual events, often held in the spring and the fall. Look for "public service" notices on television and in the newspaper and on marquee-type signs. When you're there, if appropriate, volunteer to work for next year's sale. Workers often get first pick of the merchandise.

• *Thrift shops.* The most common are the Salvation Army, Goodwill Industries, and St. Vincent de Paul stores, but many local organizations operate thrift shops as well. It pays to make friends with the workers in these stores. Often they will call you if certain items become available or new shipments come in.

• *Antique and home shows.* These are not usually a bargain-shopper's paradise, but they are a great way to see what's out there in the market and have a good time as well. Look for notices in the Sunday paper and also the calendar sections of antique-oriented magazines.

• *Antique shops and malls.* Antique stores have been around for centuries. The antique mall, in which smaller dealers rent space to show their wares, is a more recent idea. Both shops and malls tend to spring up in slightly older areas of town or outside the city limits. Restored downtown areas are a mecca for this kind of store. Some will be listed in the Yellow Pages; others you will have to find for yourself. Fortunately, they tend to stick together, so one trip may take you to several "attics." If you are traveling, you might find some of these listed in tourist brochures. Also try the "Welcome" centers at state borders or city tourist bureaus.

• *Secondhand and junk shops.* The difference between an antique shop and a junk shop is often in the eye of the beholder. Some purists say an object must predate 1830 or 1850 be to called an antique; others say it should just be old and of good workmanship. I tend toward the latter. At any rate, secondhand shops and even junk dealers can sometimes yield surprising treasure. You will have to dig deeper, but you may have more fun.

• *Flea markets.* Large outdoor and indoor flea markets are usually well advertised and marked. Look for large signs along the highway. Keep in mind, though, that "flea market" can mean anything from a big junk sale to a sophisticated antique mall and that many flea markets sell more cheap new merchandise than old treasures. They may still be fun to browse, but know what you're getting.

• *Estate sales and house sales.* These will usually be announced in the classified sections of the paper. They are often run by professionals who specialize in the liquidation of households, and they are well attended by professionals who know what they want and are ready to get it. This means you must be prepared to move fast or dig deep. Go early (some sales have you "take a number"), and take along a flashlight. Since the "nice stuff" may quickly be picked over, you may find your best treasure in an attic or basement.

• *Junkyards.* These are likely sources of tools, outdoor decorations, antique car parts, and...junk. These can often be found on old business routes and secondary highways.

• *Someone else's attic!* If you have a friend with a large house in the family, offer to help clean out the attic or basement in return for "first dibs" on any treasure you find.

What was her life like?

Was this beautiful object a treasure for her, too?

My friend Anne and her husband "adopted" their wedding rings at an antique sale with exactly that in mind. Their initial thinking in buying antique rings was to save money. But when they discovered the worn rings in the case they found themselves fantasizing about the original owners. Were they happy together? Did their marriage last? Why were their rings being sold at an antique sale? They bought the rings and still wear them with a sense of connection to a couple they will never know.

Whenever I buy and use an object that has been used before, I have the sense that I am carrying on a bit of someone's heritage, making some otherwise forgotten person part of my story and becoming part of theirs as well. I am touching something that someone before me has touched, loving what someone else has loved. And somehow, in the process, I feel we are connecting, touching hands across the silent decades.

That, to me, is the most wonderful of possibilities. In the long run, it's what keeps me in granny's attic… touching, wondering, playing, imagining.

What a perfect way to spend a rainy day.

Or, for that matter, any day.

Don't Overlook the Bits & Pieces!

The real treasures in granny's attic are the bits and pieces you can buy for pennies and then transform into real treasure in another form. Here are some ideas.

* Torn or worn linens and lace can be recycled into pictures, pillows, napkins, and clothing. Loose medallions and bits of unfinished lace can often be found for very little money.

* If you shop in granny's attic often, pick up single lids and stoppers or cruets and teapots without lids. You may find that two "orphans" fit each other. If not, crystal stoppers can be used as suncatchers or Christmas ornaments; lidless vessels can serve as vases and planters.

* Old, beat-up, gold-leaf picture frames are a prize. You can patch the molding with chewing gum and respray the gold, or you can soak the whole frame in a bathtub until the plaster comes off and refinish the beautiful pine underneath.

* Look for single, mismatched items, which are often priced lower than those in a set. Odd kitchen chairs can be refinished and combined at a table for a unique effect. Miscellaneous plates and saucers can also be combined on a table to a stunning effect.

* Old costume jewelry can be recycled and repaired. Children love it for dress-up. Sometimes you can buy a whole box from a thrift shop or secondhand store. Even broken costume jewelry can be a great resource for crafting future treasures.

* Odd drawers from broken pieces can be used as file boxes, flower boxes, baskets, spice holders, shelves, shadowboxes, letter trays—you can often get them free from dealers. Look for attractive wood in nice shapes to use as shelves, cabinets, and other fixtures.

* Be quick to pounce on cabinets, trunks, and cases that can be put to different uses. One expert combined a beat-up spice shelf with a children's tea set to make a charming miniature dish cabinet. In the same way, interesting old boards can become plate shelves or book shelves. Suitcases and baskets can hold collections. The limit is your imagination!

Old Friend Suzie: An Attic Mystery

All the years that I was growing up, a picture hung in my bedroom. It depicted two small puppies napping on a table and a tiny kitten with its smiling face raised high in between them. The caption read "Suzie." Many nights I went to sleep looking at Suzie and her companions. The frame was old and hung from a nail by twine that wrapped around two thumbtacks, one mounted in each upper corner of the frame.

When I married and left home, I left "Suzie" behind and never thought to wonder what would happen to her. She was simply part of my childhood life, along with a ship clock with tin sails I had won for selling newspaper subscriptions. After my father died, Mom had a garage sale and part of the departed treasures included "Suzie" and the clock.

Thirty-two years later I was asked to speak at a meeting some four hundred miles from home. I asked my wife, Paula, to join me on the trip, and she agreed to do so under the condition that we spend a few days afterward roaming the territory. (I'm not really much for shopping and sightseeing, but she loves to browse in old shops.)

After the meeting I was driving down a divided road in a rainstorm. Suddenly to my left I saw an antique shop that pulled at me like a magnet, tugging on me to make a U-turn and come back. This I did. As I roamed from table to table looking at all of the discarded treasure, my eye traveled to a picture leaning on a fireplace mantle. The frame was very old. The twine that hung from two corner thumbtacks was dark from years of collecting dust. And there, in the center of the picture between her two sleeping companions, was my old friend Suzie. On the same mantle sat my clock ship with its tin sails.

There was no doubt in my mind of the authenticity of my find! The merchant made a sale, and I then realized the meaning of the phrase, "one man's junk is another man's treasure." In this case, a timeless treasure because all those years in between faded quickly and, for a brief moment, I was that ten-year-old looking at my smiling friend Suzie, which I still cherish to this day.

—Kenneth Barnes (my brother-in-law),
Palm Springs, California

Give her of the fruit of her hands;
and let her own works praise her in the gates.

—THE BOOK OF PROVERBS

Lovingly Crafted

THE JOY OF HANDMADE TREASURES

HANDMADE.

The very word says treasure.

And how much more precious that word becomes when it names an object crafted by someone we love.

Handmade treasures carry that special glow because they represent an extra investment of time and personality. It's almost as if the soul of the maker has time to rub off during those hours of planning and dreaming, stitching and cutting, whittling and sanding and painting.

When you touch a handmade treasure, in a sense you're touching the hands and heart of the maker—and that's true whether or not you have personally met that person. You're touching the joy of inspiration, the sacrifice of time and energy, the pain of pricked fingers and smashed thumbs, the determination to persevere, the hope of producing something beautiful and lasting and useful.

Every handmade treasure you hold in your hand represents, to one degree or another, an investment of love. And that, of course, is what makes you touch it so tenderly.

The quilt an elderly aunt painstakingly stitched out of pieces of your old dresses.

The needlepoint Christmas stocking your mother stitched for you when your brother wasn't even born yet.

The crooked potholders your six-year-old nephew created yesterday on his little square loom.

Or the scarf you've been knitting to give your husband. Yes, the work of your hands is a treasure, too.

What you create today is tomorrow's heirloom—your personal contribution to the world of timeless treasures. And it's just as precious an investment as the quaint work of yesterday's craftsperson. If anything, it's more precious because today's handmade treasures ask a more deliberate sacrifice. In a world where time daily grows scarcer and hurry dominates our lives, we must *choose* to invest our time and our hearts and our hands in the service of love.

In the "olden days" when men sat on the porch in the evenings and whittled, when quilting and embroidery were among the few available forms of entertainment, when making something by hand was the only way to attain it, handcrafted items were an inevitable by-product of everyday life. They, too, required sacrifice, for making something beautiful took time away from the life-or-death business of living. In another sense, however, making things by hand was business as usual.

Today, for most of us, making something by hand is entirely optional. We don't need to sew or weave in order to have clothes to wear. We don't need to quilt or knit or crochet in order to have warm blankets. We don't need to whittle and hammer and saw in order to have houses to live in and furniture to sit on.

Today, choosing to making something by hand often means a conscious sacrifice of leisure time. You are choosing to quilt or sand or paint when you could be watching TV or going to the mall. You are making a deliberate investment of yourself for the sake of the future—for the sake of love.

There are compensations, of course. Working with one's hands can be deeply satisfying. What a joy it is to produce something useful, something beautiful, something that memories can attach themselves to.

I've never heard anyone complain, "I wish I hadn't wasted so much time making that hand-carved wooden trunk. I could have watched TV instead!"

And don't make the mistake of assuming that today's handmade treasures "just won't be as nice" as somebody made long ago. You may not be a professional artist, but neither were

An Edible Heirloom

This old-fashioned traditional wedding cake recipe has been in my husband's family for generations. Every time a family member got married, my husband's grandmother (best known as "Gram") and the other ladies of the family would get together to make this *very* special and *delicious* cake. Though Gram went to be with the Lord many years ago, we feel she *is* with us every time our family prepares this timeless cake. The following is adapted from the recipe Gram gave me years ago to store in my recipe collection.

GRAM LOIS PEARSON'S WEDDING CAKE

2 ¾ cups flour
4 teaspoons baking powder
½ teaspoon salt
1 cup shortening
2 cups sugar
½ cup milk
½ cup water
1 teaspoon lemon extract
1 teaspoon vanilla
6 egg whites (large)

Sift together flour, baking powder, and salt. In another bowl, cream together sugar and shortening.

Blend milk, water, and extracts, then add half of this mixture to the sugar/shortening mixture along with some of the dry ingredients. Blend with electric mixer (or by hand, as Gram did) until smooth. Continue mixing in a balance of wet and dry ingredients. Add egg whites last, mixing well until batter looks fluffy. Bake in two greased and floured nine-inch cake pans at 350 degrees for 35-40 minutes. Cool and ice. Cake freezes very well, so can be made ahead of time, then iced and decorated later.

FROSTING

3 cups sifted powdered sugar
½ teaspoon cream of tartar
pinch of salt
6 tablespoons shortening
1 teaspoon lemon extract
1 egg white (large)
water to thin

Sift powdered sugar with cream of tartar and salt into medium bowl. Add shortening, lemon extract, and egg white. Blend until smooth, thinning only as necessary with water (adding small amounts to obtain desired consistency). Note: A butter-cream frosting of your choice may be substituted for this original "stiff" frosting. To add ornamental roses or designs, please consult any cookbook or cake decorating book.

most of the people whose handiwork we cherish today as antiques.

The embroidered sheets that were part of your great-aunt's hope chest are fully as precious as the Whistler portrait that hangs in someone else's living room. The little wooden animals your great-uncle whittled for your cousin many years ago are fully as precious as the Rodin sculpture in someone's garden. And your son's or daughter's third-grade masterpiece is as worthy of being a treasure as the art in a national gallery.

Handmade treasure doesn't have to be expertly wrought to be precious. It is valuable for what it is—an expression of a unique personality and an offering of love.

Think of how you treasure your children's art. The lopsided clay flower pots and the crayoned papers have a value to you far out of proportion to their technical merit. You save them and preserve them for the love they represent, for the growing personality they echo, for the memories they recall.

And that—beyond the intrinsic workmanship—is the value of any handmade treasure. It shows a personality at work, a consciousness making its mark on the world.

My own heritage includes a treasury of handmade needlework. My mother and my aunts were a tailor's daughters, and they were all expert seamstresses. My earliest memories are of my mother at her sewing machine or sitting in her wing chair doing handwork. She taught me to stitch and knit and embroider. Those skills in themselves are a timeless treasure! We spent many quiet evenings on our work. I still have some tea towels we embroidered together, and I use and treasure those simple handmade treasures for the memories they bring me.

In recent years, my writing and speaking schedule has limited my sewing time, but I have always managed to make something for the grandbabies when they arrived. Simple "blankies" of soft flannel edged in satin provide a comforting touch, and these small handmade treasures are kept and treasured for many years. (When the children get a little older, I like to make them car blankets or little quilts with pockets in the corners so they can tuck their feet in for warmth.)

> Enough,
> if something
> from our hands
> has power to
> live, and act,
> and serve the
> future hour.
>
> —WILLIAM WORDSWORTH

When our oldest granddaughter, Christine, was born, her handmade blankie was simply a ten-inch flannel square. The pink silk binding matched the tiny pink roses in the flannel. Christine became solidly attached to that blankie. As she grew older, she gradually undid a corner of the silk. She would twist it around her fingers in a little loop, feel the silk, and suck her thumb. Finally, when Christine was seven or eight, it was time for the blankie to be put away. Christine did it herself. She took her blankie and put it in an envelope and stored it away, although sometimes she would go and look at it.

Now Christine is thirteen years old. I was shopping this Christmas and came across a teapot that had little pink roses. She absolutely loved it. I said, "Go find me your blankie." The roses on the blankie and the roses on the teapot matched exactly! For her birthday this year I plan to put her blankie in a frame so she can hang it near her teapot as a memory of love and comfort.

> *The artist, like the God of the creation, remains within or behind or beyond or above his handiwork.*
>
> —JAMES JOYCE

I learned the art of blankie-making from my mother, who used to make three or four at a time and save them to give as baby gifts. When Mama died, I found three or four little flannel blankies she had made, along with a couple of little rattles. At that time, my oldest grandchildren were past the baby stage, so I saved those blankets for a few years. Then, when little Bradley Joe was born to our son, Brad, and his wife, Maria, I wrapped up a blankie and a rattle with a note: "For your firstborn from Grandma Irene. She would have loved to give this to you yourself." Brad, who loved his grandmother very much, wept when they opened that package. Maria understood his feelings and has made a point of using that little blanket all the time. Whenever I see it, I am touched to see my mama's handiwork in the chubby little hands of a great-grandson she never met.

Handmade treasures don't have to be dainty and soft, like a baby's blankie, to be loved. We once stayed with a family in Kansas City, Missouri, whose beloved treasure was a massive, sturdy swing set. The father built it when the children were small. The children played on it growing up, and, as they grew older, they would go out and sit on the swings when they needed to think. Once, when the family needed to move, the kids balked because they didn't want to leave their swing set. So they moved the swing—taking it apart and numbering the pieces for reassembly. Now the kids have all left the nest and the parents have retired, but their neatly manicured lawn still sports that beloved swing set. The parents swear that when the kids come home, the best talks still take place on the old swings.

My Dream Bed

Growing up in my home I graduated from a baby bed to a bunkbed to a double bed. Nothing fancy, mostly just functional. I always dreamed about a pretty bedroom and then it happened. My mother gave me a beautiful heirloom bed. It had been given to her by an uncle who had inherited it himself. My dream bed was handmade and carved by my great-great grandfather who was an immigrant from Germany.

My bed followed me to my first home as a married woman, and it now presides as the focal point of our guest room. My bed is meaningful to me because the man who made it came from Germany five generations ago, with little more than he could carry. It is a privilege to possess one of the handcrafted pieces of furniture he used in his new home in his new country.

—Pat A. Guthrie, Humboldt, Tennessee

Quilted Memories

When my grandmother was eighty years old, she made me a quilt out of scraps of material left over from her sewing projects of many years. Her aprons are in it, housedresses, curtains, couch slipcovers, my aunt's dresses. She made it with love. It was the first of just two she ever made—the other quilt was for my sister. She said it was something she always wanted to make. She did something new at such an advanced age!

Grandma died a month after my daughter was born, at age ninety-eight. But each time I look at that quilt, I think of who Grandma was, how I loved her and she loved me, and I recall her dresses, aprons, furniture, curtains, outfits she made for me—her world and her home.

—*Lorraine Lee, Fremont, California*

In a sense, a handmade treasure doesn't even have to be handmade! One father I know regularly makes audiotapes to mail to his children. One offering was simply a reading of poems he had written, along with explanations about the background of each. Another tape was a "live recording" of the family's Christmas morning gathering—complete with a spirited rendition of "The Night Before Christmas."

These audio treasures have been listened to many times with great delight, and they have been copied several times to guard against deterioration. Although the father did not personally craft the plastic covers and the magnetic tape, his "handmade" (or perhaps heartmade) offerings are truly timeless treasures to those who love him.

Lovingly prepared cooking can be a handcrafted treasure! The actual food quickly becomes a memory, but the recipes and the skills survive to be passed down from generation to generation.

One of my favorite and most-used treasures is a little recipe book Bob's mother compiled many years ago for my sister-in-law and me. She wrote down all the recipes our husbands had loved best: main dishes, desserts, jams and jellies—even her famous chili. I have long cherished the generosity of that gift, for she was giving away something she could have kept to herself. She was giving me the power to nurture and cherish her son. In the process, she was also giving me a piece of herself. And that is what makes her little book such a timeless treasure to me.

It is the person behind any handmade object that makes it such a treasure.

It may be dainty and delicate (like a linen dresser scarf) or homely and comforting (like a patchwork quilt) or brawny and assertive (like a floor-to-ceiling cabinet).

It may have survived centuries, or it may have been made yesterday.

It may be meticulously stitched, expertly carved, brilliantly conceived, simply beautiful. Or it may be simple or flawed, the creation of clumsy fingers and a loving heart.

No matter what it looks like, a handmade treasure is precious because it carries the soul of its maker in its very molecules. Its message to us is the same one that used to be embroidered on friendship quilts and carefully inscribed in autograph books—a message that is both a plea and a blessing.

"When this you see," it says to us, "remember me."

A Taste of My Treasure

Gertie Barnes, my special mother-in-law, is famous for her chili. That's why I consider it such a gift that she shared the recipe with me early in my marriage—so I could make it for our Bob. Now she's willing to share it with you, too. If you like spicy food, you'll love this edible treasure!

GRANDMA GERTIE'S TEXAS CHILI

3 pounds ground round (or ground turkey)
2 eight-ounce cans tomato sauce
⅓ cup chili powder
3 tablespoons onions flakes

7 cloves garlic, chopped
4 cans water
1 tablespoon oregano
2½ teaspoons cumin
½ to 2 teaspoons crushed red pepper (or more)
2 tablespoons paprika
1½ teaspoons salt or to taste

Sear meat until grayish in color, not brown. Add rest of ingredients. Cover kettle and let simmer 2 hours, stirring occasionally. Taste for meat tenderness and seasoning. Serves a crowd (at least 12) and freezes well for future use.

Something That Lasts

I've been a hard worker all my life,
but 'most all my work has been
the kind that "perishes with the
usin'," as the Bible says.
That's the discouragin' thing
about a woman's work . . . .
If a woman was to see all the
dishes that she had to wash before
she died, piled up before her in one
pile, she'd lie down and die right
then and there.
I've always had the name o' bein'
a good housekeeper,
but when I'm dead and gone there
ain't anybody goin' to think o'
the floors I've swept,
and the tables I've scrubbed,
and the old clothes I've patched,
and the stockin's I've darned. . . .
But when one of my grandchildren
or great-grandchildren
sees one o' these quilts,
they'll think about Aunt Jane,
and, wherever I am then,
I'll know I ain't forgotten.

—ELIZA CALVERT,
AUNT JANE OF KENTUCKY

But I Don't Sew!

WHAT TO DO WHEN YOU CAN'T MAKE IT YOURSELF

If you are handy with a needle or a paintbrush or a circle saw, you probably don't need to be encouraged to create a handmade treasure. But what do you do if your skills or your schedule or your patience level tells you that a hand-stitched quilt or a hand-thrown pot or a hand-carved creche is just not a possibility in the near future? Be encouraged. If you have a heart for handmade treasures, it's easy to have it in your life as well. Here are some suggestions.

• *Pay tribute to local artists or craftspersons by investing in their work.* Instead of hanging a poster or a print from a department store, hang a signed, numbered print or a stained-glass window made by an artist at a craft fair or art co-op. Look for someone whose work you love but who is relatively unknown. Save the paperwork just in case that artist becomes famous some day!

• *Commission a handmade treasure from an elderly relative.* You supply the yarn or fabric (and perhaps the company) and she supplies the skill. Better yet, ask her to teach you! The craft of tatting or whittling passed on from one generation to the next is a true timeless treasure.

• *Rescue handmade treasures from flea markets and thrift shops.* Use them in a way that gives homage to their craftsmanship. Use as intended (a hankie as a hankie, a napkin as a napkin) or be creative. Two embroidered dresser scarves crisscrossed over a square table makes a wonderful place setting for four.

• *Trade a favor with a talented friend.* You clean her house; she makes you a set of handwoven placemats or a batik vest.

• *Take a class and learn to make something!* Have you always wanted to do calligraphy, pottery, or weaving? You can find someone to teach you at your local community college or recreational center. Your local craft store is bulging with projects that are easy to learn and make.

• *Remember that there are other ways to create timeless treasure besides carving and needlepoint.* Can you play the piano or sing lullabies on tape? Can you write a children's story and hire a desktop publisher to print and bind it? Produce a family video?

The Gift of Teaching

The original price of 10¢ is stamped on my timeless treasure. I don't know when my grandmother bought her little stainless-steel crochet hook or if it was passed down to her as it was to me. I've often wondered what her thoughts were as she created the dainty gifts for her family and friends with that tiny tool. The many hours of use are still quite evident, as there is a slight curve in the neck of the slender size 9 hook.

I was not a recipient of any of those beautiful gifts that my grandmother made, but I have seen several of them. Instead of the finished product, I received the tool that was used to make them. It was given to me by my mother. Along with the crochet hook came the joy of learning from her how to use it. My goal was to make a doily. Mom made one right along with me as I learned the stitches, took out rows, and compared progress. She not only taught me the skill that was passed down to her from her mother, but she shared her heart. I learned about bits of her childhood that helped me to know her mother, this grandmother who had died before I was old enough to really know and remember her. She shared a part of herself as she passed along to me the skill and the treasured tool.

Yes, I wonder if my grandmother ever thought that her tiny crochet hook would someday belong to her granddaughter along with the joy that she herself must have known as she used it. I'm so thankful for my timeless treasure and the treasured time with my mom. My hope is to pass on this little hook, the skill of using it, and some treasured time to a granddaughter of my own someday.

—*Connie Taylor, Chehalis, Washington*

Be My Treasured Valentine

I want to tell you about the Valentine my darling daddy made for me when I was a little girl. It was during the Great Depression, and I believe I was six or seven years old.

It was Valentine's Day and I came home from school with a big red paper heart (undoubtedly embellished with a paper lace doily!) and a carefully printed "To Daddy."

We lived on a large citrus ranch and we only "went to town" on Saturday afternoons, so there was no quick trip to the Hallmark store that afternoon for my dad. Instead, my soft-hearted father made me a Valentine of wood!

As I look at it now, I am so impressed at how creative he was! With just a scrap of wood, two crayons, and a knife, he made my "timeless treasure."

It is one of my most cherished keepsakes, as you can imagine.

—*Carol Farmer, San Ramon, California*

769/500

I'll note you in my book of memory.

—WILLIAM SHAKESPEARE

The Gift of Memory

KEEPING LOVE AND HISTORY ALIVE

I HAVE GIVEN MANY GIFTS to my children and grandchildren and nieces and nephews over the years.

I suspect I will give many more before my life is through.

Some will be simple, some extravagant, most carefully chosen, a few picked up in haste on the way to a birthday party. Some may be rare and unusual, the kind of gift that makes the giver hover excitedly while the paper is unwrapped.

But even those incomparable treasures could have been uncovered by someone else—even, heaven forbid, by another grandmother. They're unusual, but they're not unique.

There's only one gift in all the world that can be given by me alone, only one gift I can give that is truly unique.

That is the gift of my memories, captured and preserved and passed on to the people I love. Only I can preserve the timeless treasure of what I have lived, what I have experienced, what I have loved and learned. And this is the treasure that conveys my heart and my love to them most eloquently.

Even the treasures that I make by hand, the blankets and the pillows and the toys, provide a mute testimony to my love for them. These things may add warmth and (I hope) beauty to their lives. They extend my touch to places where I can't be. But not even the most exquisite handmade treasures can communicate the way a picture can. The way a word can.

Sometimes you have to tell the story by actually telling the story.

And the gift of family stories preserved in words and pictures is an irreplaceable treasure.

How many of us, faced with the classic question of what we would grab from a burning building, would answer, "The photo albums!" Pictures tell a story in a way that teacups and tablecloths simply cannot.

And yet even photos lose their memory. Have you had the experience of unearthing a pile of pictures and discovering you have no idea who those people are? Have you ever turned over a lively, intriguing snapshot only to stare at a blank back? Who is that man with Aunt Rosie? Was she ever that skinny? And where was I when that picture was taken?

All of which brings us back to words, which are the most dependable preservers of stories. That's why I believe our stories put into words are among the most valuable treasures we can leave behind us.

I'll never forget one evening long ago, when we went to the house of one of Jenny's boyfriends for din-

ner. The occasion was a birthday of some sort, and the boy's grandmother was there. At that family celebration, as they did at every family celebration, the young people pulled up a rocker and sat Grandma down in it and sat on the floor around her. "Okay, Grandma," they said, "tell us the stories." And that lucky woman sat in her rocker amid a circle of lucky teenagers and started telling them the stories she had told since they were small, the stories they knew by heart.

That was a beautiful evening. The grandmother was giving her grandchildren a beautiful gift of her memories, and they were giving her the gift of their attention and interest. I've thought of that evening often when I've told stories to my own grandchildren.

And yet, wouldn't it be even more wonderful if someone had thought to write those stories down or turn on a tape recorder—capturing not only the stories but

the beloved grandmother's voice and her unique turns of phrase? Wouldn't it be a treasure to be able to hear those stories again just as she told them, to feel the touch of her spirit in a more direct way for many years to come?

I have been working on this for quite a few years now. I've consciously set out to become an archivist, a preserver of story-treasures I hope my grandchildren will remember. I believe it is one of the best ways any of us can pass along treasure to our children.

So how do you preserve your story-treasures?

The method depends on your gifts and interests.

The very simplest form is simply taking the time to write down names and dates that might be forgotten.

You may cringe at the thought of writing your autobiography or even a memory of a childhood incident, but you can pull out that box of photographs and label them. You can write down names and dates in the family Bible. You can keep a scrapbook of special events in your life or your children's lives.

When my children graduated from high school, I prepared a

> *I have written my life in small sketches, a little today, a little yesterday, as I have thought of it, as I remember all the things from childhood on through the years, good ones, and unpleasant ones, that is how they come out and that is how we have to take them.*
>
> —ANNA MARY MOSES (GRANDMA MOSES)

"This Is Your Life" album for each of them. I bought a scrapbook and decorated the cover, then filled the books with memorabilia I had saved—from birth announcements to graduation pictures. Report cards, hand-drawn pictures, invitations to important parties, photos of friends, even letters they had written from camp—all these things told the stories of their lives up until then.

My children enjoyed their books when I gave them to them, but none of us had any idea how much they would use those books in years to come. Even now they refer to their books for names and dates. They "borrow" baby pictures to take to parties. They entertain their children with this evidence that they were once children themselves.

Encouraged by the success of those books, I dug back into my personal archives and made books for Bob and me as well. And, in the process, I learned so much about who we are and where we came from. Even a recent excursion through "my book" brought me a renewed sense of my mother's character. In a handwritten note to a teacher on one of my old report cards, I saw again my mother's humble and gracious spirit.

I cherish that note, along with the other items I have saved that have my mother and father's handwriting on them. There is something so very personal about those handwritten mementos; they bring my par-

A House Full of Memories

I've often said that my ideal home is not one full of new things, but one filled with memories wherever you look.

The secretary from my grandmother's home stirs up the most memories for me. Every time I look at that piece of furniture, I think of her. Family was important to Grammie. She was boarded out for much of her childhood and she was determined to provide a loving and stable home for her own children. That love and care just kept right on coming to her grandchildren and great-grandchildren, and, I might add, to anyone else who needed a place to stay or a warm meal.

I've often thought how pleased Grammie would be if she could see her secretary now. It holds pictures of four generations of her family, including the great-great granddaughter that she never got to see. The section of the secretary that held Grammie's books is mostly used as her china cabinet was used. On the shelf sit a few cups and saucers, some odds and ends, and a newly purchased child's bunny tea set.

Grammie's secretary reminds me of the special bond that can exist between grandmother and granddaughter. Now, it's my turn to be the grandmother. What a privilege I have to be able to pass on not only Grammie's furniture to future generations, but also her love.

—**Linda S. Mitchell, Edmonds, Washington**

"I am not a writer, and this is not book. . . ."

That's how my grandmother began the short memoir she put together for the family several years before she died. She wrote it with a ballpoint in her beautifully legible teacher's handwriting. I then typed it on a word processor (which I was just learning to use) and made copies for her to give as Christmas gifts. My copy, in its simple cardboard binder, is inscribed to me with a "Merry Christmas." I have tucked the original handwritten manuscript inside the cover.

Actually, I am blessed to own copies of a number of family documents, including the memoirs of an ancestor who was a child during the Revolutionary War, my great-great grandfather's Civil War diary, and the written memories of two great-aunts. But my grandmother's story means the most to me because I spent so much time with her when I was little.

My daughter Elizabeth was only three when Mammaw died, and she doesn't really remember her. But I have read my grandmother's little "nonbook" to her as a bedtime story. She loved hearing about how her little great-grandma Ella Josephine, waded into a creek to escape a spanking, ate roasted sweet potatoes as "candy," and talked her way into college at age sixteen. Reading it to my daughter, I was once more impressed by the courage and determination of a little girl who "always wanted to be an explorer."

When my daughter is older, she will have her own copy of her great-grandmother's memoir. She can put it on the shelf with her own treasure . . . a collection of "Elizabethan sonnets" that her own granddad wrote for her.

—Anne Christian Buchanan, Knoxville, Tennessee

ents so much closer to me. I can well understand why people have told me that a loved-one's Bible, with passages underlined and notes scribbled in the margin, is a timeless treasure. A handwritten remembrance writes something special in our hearts.

So, I have made a point to leave my children that kind of personal, handwritten treasure from me. Every year on our vacation, for instance, I sit down and write each of my grown children a letter. While I relax by the pool or on the beach, I pull out my stationery and tell them just how much I love them. I write about how excited I was when they were born. I relive favorite memories of them as children. I applaud their efforts to be good parents and tell them what a great job I think they are doing.

I have no idea whether these letters are timeless treasures to my children. They have thanked me for sending them, but we've never discussed the contents. Nevertheless, I continue to write them. They are my way of giving them my love and encouragement in tangible form. I suspect they will mean more in the future than they do now.

Another woman I know has made a practice of sharing a "note book" with her eight-year-old daughter. In a blank book with gilt edges, they take turns writing messages and leave it for the other to find. The book will appear on the daughter's bed with a note of encouragement after school. Then it will find its way, along with an answer, to the mother's desk. The purpose of this exercise in correspondence, in the mother's mind, is to create a way of communicating with her daughter during times when talking is difficult. But in the process they are also creating a timeless treasure that captures the little girl's changing handwriting and the

A Family Frame

I have a picture hanging in my living room that is my timeless treasure and was made from the following.

My great grandmother Susie Hash handmade a double wedding-ring quilt from scraps of material she used to sew her children and grandchildren's clothes. A piece of this quilt serves as the backdrop.

A dress, resembling a christening gown, worn by my paternal grandfather, Omen Hash, rests atop the quilt.

Atop the dress is an old photo of my great-grandmother Susie Hash, my paternal grandfather, Omen Hash, my paternal great-uncle, Lunus Hash, and a spinster great-great-aunt who lived in the home and helped care for the children and the house (name unavailable).

These treasures were framed in an old family frame (more than a hundred years old) and given to me by my maternal great-aunt, May Galloway, thus creating the union of two families.

I look at this picture every day and am reminded of the love I have been fortunate to receive throughout my life.

—*Darcy Oliveira, Visalia, California*

mother's ongoing dreams.

Letter writing is a wonderful way of building relationships while preserving our words for future generations. So is the practice of keeping diaries and journals. In fact, much of what we know about previous generations comes from these priceless written sources.

We give a gift of memory to the next generation when we keep a chronicle of our everydays. By the discipline of recording our thoughts and observations, we capture those tiny experiences that may shape us almost without being noticed. In the process, we provide a picture for posterity of what it was like to live an ordinary life in our particular day and age.

When we were visiting my Bob's mother just a few weeks ago, she surprised us with a journal that her mother had kept back in 1964. We sat on the bed in the bedroom and read through it, going back in time to those days when Grandma White was still alive. We found our own names in there, and we were amazed to find that one year we visited her at least seven times. We have no memory of going by that much. And we had no idea of how much it meant to her. Just reading through that journal made us feel connected again to that sweet woman who taught my Bob so much. We were grateful for the chance to share her memories, which otherwise would have been forgotten. And we were grateful to Bob's mother, Gertie, for bothering to keep that precious record.

Preserving a written memory takes time and space and effort. Tasks like labeling photos and making scrapbooks and writing down stories, of course, are the ones that fall by the wayside in the mad rush of day-to-day living. How many parents have discovered that

> *Even if your life story is not intended for a commercial publisher and is not the stuff of gossip columns or heroic achievements, the experiences you have had are your own greatest treasure, well worth the remembering and retelling.*
>
> —RAY MUNGO

A Photographic Memory

Pictures have become very meaningful to me, including my parents' wedding pictures and my own wedding picture. I hadn't realized until a relative gave me pictures from my parents' wedding day that the necklace my mother wore—the one she gave to me with no information about its history—I also wore at my wedding twenty years later!

My parents were divorced when I was young, and these pictures helped me piece together the past. I have also gathered together pictures of my grandparents and relatives when they were children.

One of my favorite combinations of photographs is one of my husband Bob's mother on her high school graduation, Bob's graduation picture, and our son Erik's graduation picture. Also a combination of my wedding picture, my parents' wedding picture, and Bob's parents' wedding picture.

As I busy myself at my tasks and focus on these years in my life, my photographs remind me that there is so much more to life than just today!

—Nan Simonsen, Riverside, California

the second child's (or even the first one's) baby book never gets completed, that the little envelopes of photos get stashed in drawers, that years slip by and memories grow stale?

I know. It happens to me, too. And there is a sense in which the business of daily living must take precedence over recording and archiving it.

And yet I know that the stories that are remembered are the stories that get told. The stories that are written or taped are the ones that become timeless treasures.

And don't fool yourself. The experience or insight that rings so bright in your memory today can be gone tomorrow. Memories can be more vulnerable to time's ravages than the most delicate glassware.

There are so many tales my mother and my aunts told me that have already dimmed in my memory. There are so many stories about my mother's childhood in Brooklyn, about her early married life, about her experiences as a costumer in Hollywood, that I wish I could pull up from the edges of my consciousness. She told me once, and I've all but forgotten . . . and she's not here to ask anymore.

> *Honor your own stories and tell them too. The tales may not seem very important, but they are what binds families and makes each of us who we are.*
>
> —MADELEINE L'ENGLE

Always Connected

I could tell stories about the antique bride doll that my mom got on her tenth birthday and gave to me on my tenth birthday, or about our picture wall that tells the story of our family tree through photographs that are over one hundred years old. And I could tell about all of the documents that my great-grandfather gave me before he died that tell our family tree back to the 1600s. But I want to tell about something that means more to me than anything in the world.

When I was eleven years old, my parents separated. It was a complex, messy situation and so, for my benefit, they sent me to live with my grandparents. I was brokenhearted. I refused to go to school or do anything but sit on the couch and watch TV. Sometimes I would just sit there and cry.

One day my grandpa walked in with a stack of paper and a pair of scissors. He folded the paper like a fan and started cutting furiously. When he finished he had a string of paper dolls, all of them holding hands. He held them up to me and told me something that touched my heart and continues to hold me together at times. He said, "You see how these little dolls are all attached together? They are attached because they are family. No matter what comes between them, they are still going to be attached because they are family. Just like your mom and dad—there are things that have happened between them, but they will always be your mom and dad and you will always be attached together by love."

My grandpa died not long after that, but my paper dolls are here, ten years later, to remind me that no matter what—even in the separation of death—love and family will always keep us connected.

—*Christine E. Prentice, Apple Valley, California*

A Christmas Memory

Christmas or other holidays provide wonderful opportunities for recording treasured memories. (Dylan Thomas's *A Child's Christmas in Wales* is delightful.) My husband, Bob, wrote this brief account of a special Christmas in his own life. Why not write down one of your own Christmas memories as a gift for your family?

The Christmas I was nine years old, my family was new in Southern California. Dad had hitchhiked west to take a new job his older brother had found for him. Then Mom and my brothers and I had come out on the train, making the big move from a small farming community in New Mexico to the big city of Los Angeles.

It was a wonderful new start for our family, but Christmas wasn't going to be so wonderful. With a new home, a new job, and moving expenses, there was simply no money for Christmas presents. Mom and Dad informed us early in the season so we wouldn't get our hopes up for a new bicycle, toys, or even new clothes. I understood, sort of. But on Christmas Eve, before going to sleep, I prayed, "Lord, somehow could You just send a little gift for Christmas morning? Thank You for Your help! Amen!"

I woke bright and early. Just as we had been warned, there were no presents anywhere. Our family had breakfast, but still no gifts. Had my prayer made no difference?

About nine o'clock I saw a black Buick sedan rolling slowly down our small, narrow street. As the car got closer I recognized my dad's brother, Uncle Bernice. He pulled up in front of our house, climbed out of his car, then pulled out a mysterious box, which he carried into the house.

Sure enough, Uncle Bernice had brought one gift apiece for each of my two brothers and me. Mine was a bow and arrow set. I was so thrilled to have that one gift on a Christmas when I was afraid there would be nothing. As I went to bed that evening, I looked to the ceiling and said, "Thank You, God, for listening to a little nine-year-old boy."

The older I become, the more I am aware of the memory treasures that seem to flit out of my reach. And, as years go by, the people who can help me remember are slipping away. How I wish we had more letters and diaries and tapes and Bibles and autobiographies that could answer our questions and shape our thinking. How grateful I am that somebody thought to do an oral history on tape with Bob's father before he died!

Author Alex Haley once said that whenever an old person dies, it's as if a book has been removed from a library. And I believe that's true.

Each person's life is important. Each person's memory enriches our heritage. Each person's story is a timeless treasure that will be lost unless someone, somewhere takes the time to preserve it.

That's true of you, too, and the people you love.

So pick up a pen. Run to the computer. Dig out your old tape recorder or your videocamera. Pull out that box of photos.

Take the time now to preserve a truly timeless treasure.

The Write Stuff

• *Use tools you feel comfortable with.* Pen, pencil, or computer; legal pad or looseleaf notebook. An old-fashioned paper and pen work beautifully, and a handwritten manuscript often has special value to future generations.

• *Don't worry about style.* Just write the way you talk. Your natural expression will be a treasure for those who come after you. If you want to, you can go back and revise or get help for grammar and spelling, but it's not necessary.

• *Be honest.* You might not choose to tell every detail, but try not to perpetuate fantasies or lies. Remember to be gentle. There is really no point in calling names or perpetuating old feuds.

• *Include dates and places.* If you don't write down these details, those who come after you may never know them.

• *Include details and feelings.* Don't let your story be a dry recital of events. Describe the dust in the road while you waited for the bus. Tell about your loneliness your first night away from home.

• *Tell about the times.* If possible, relate what happened in your personal life to what was happening in the world—it may not be obvious to someone much younger.

• *Don't be afraid to say what you think, what you've learned, to share your wisdom.* Those who come after you will appreciate it. And don't be afraid to be funny!

• *Get help if you need it.* Libraries and community colleges offer excellent resources to those who want to write their memoirs. Even better, ask a writer in your family to work with you on this project.

• *Read other autobiographies.* You will be surprised by how much they help you remember your own past.

To my friend —

Flowers will fade
away will soon
decay
Let our friendship
fade so fast
But lets forever last

*All good collectors know the very finest things
in life are well worth the effort.*

—MARYANNE DOLAN

To See and to Touch

PRESERVING YOUR TREASURES WITHOUT HIDING THEM

❧

AGING IS THE WAY OF ALL FLESH —and of all paper, wood, cloth, and iron. All material things, including your timeless treasures and mine, are vulnerable. Fabric fades. Paper crumbles. Glass shatters. Iron rusts. Thieves break through and steal.

Does that mean we should lock our treasures up tight to keep anything from happening to them?

No!

In fact, just the opposite is true.

The vast majority of your treasures are happier and healthier living with you, where you can see and enjoy them, than they are stored away. They are preserved better through use rather than through neglect.

And even if they weren't, what's the point of owning a treasure you can't enjoy? And what's the point in passing it on without the stories of living attached to it?

Treasures are treasures, remember, because of the memories and the history that go along with them. And I believe we do best by them when we continue to add rich layers to that patina of memory.

So don't hide away your treasures. Instead, enjoy them. Share them with guests. Share them with family. Touch them often.

With care, of course.

But with love, not nervousness.

And with basic precautions taken and common sense applied, there is simply no reason to lock all your treasures away in cabinets and trunks. Your timeless treasures will bring you the greatest joy if you keep them out to touch and rearrange and tell stories about.

I love the creative ways my friend Yolie uses her handkerchief collection, which was a bequest from her beloved grandmother. When you visit Yolie's house, you see her hankies draped over lamps and tied around pillows. If she serves you a cup of tea, she may place a pretty hankie between the cup and the saucer or tuck one into a silver ring to use as a napkin. The oldest and most precious of her collection she stores carefully in drawers, but she's quick to bring them out and share—and to tell their stories.

When the grandmother of a friend of mine moved into a nursing home, my friend traveled to help clean out the house. Among the treasures she brought back with her was an inexpensive decorated water glass, the kind with little decals on it. That glass was special because my friend remembered drinking from it whenever she visited. So she brought it home and put it, not in her china hutch, but in the cabinet with all the other glasses she uses every day. She often sets it at her daughter's place during meals. To her, using that glass is the best way to keep her connection with her grandmother real and tangible, and she wants to keep that connection alive for her daughter as well. She has resisted suggestions that she should pack it away.

It's not a forgotten heirloom gathering dust on a shelf. It's a timeless treasure that is busy gathering new meaning and new associations.

We use our treasures in our house, too. Bob's collection of birdhouses hang out among our trees, many with birds in them. My father's chef knife and his ladle hang in my kitchen, handy for cooking and cutting as well as remembering.

If I want to use an antique dresser scarf to line a tray, I don't dig in a box in the garage; I just open a drawer in the kitchen.

I stack my collection of quilts—the ones that are not on the beds—under a table in our great room. Sometimes I drape a quilt on the stair banisters. Sometimes I will carry one out to a garden chair on a sunny but chilly day and curl up with a book.

I keep my collection of children's books on a shelf in the guest room, where overnight visitors can flip through and enjoy them. Often a grandchild will fetch one for me to read. Visiting children often play with the dainty miniature tea sets that live on a table in our child-sized loft.

And in our house, the teacups and teaspoons and tea paraphernalia that make up my collection are simply everywhere—overflowing the shelved armoire that is their headquarters to perch on tables and cabinets, hang in cupboards, and nestle on trays. When the grandchildren come over, we drink tea from them; I have even had tea parties with a two-year-old boy and a bone-china teacup (and no tragedies).

I have found that children are amazingly respectful of my prized possessions. They understand treasures, and they have their own. When given a chance, they appreciate the honor of being allowed to look and touch . . . carefully . . . especially if a story goes with the viewing. In the process, they learn the secrets of appreciating valuable and delicate things.

I truly believe that children grow by being entrusted with treasure. I think we all do. I also believe my treasures are better off when they are surrounded by everyday living, not tucked away in a drawer or cabinet. I know I am better off for having them around me. I am infinitely happier and more productive when I am surrounded by beauty and memories.

> *Maybe you'll turn Grandma's vase into a lamp. Maybe you'll use a treasured porcelain compote as a place for potpourri. Maybe you'll pull your tea set out from under wraps. Or display your collection of clay circus animals. Or line up your wooden Noah's Ark on your bookshelf. In other words, let yourself show!*
>
> —CHARLOTTE MOSS

The Most Treasured Treasure

As the youngest of seven children, it was always my job to set the table. On special occasions, my mother would very carefully take down the special china and crystal from the top shelves of the china closet and hand them to me. She touched the pieces with such reverence and gentleness. Each item had a special story that made their first owners—the grandmother, great-grandmother, and great-great-grandmother I never knew—come alive for me. I tell those same stories to my young niece as I teach her to set the table. Now I have a new story to add to the collection.

It wasn't until I was an adult that I noticed one simple cut-glass dish was different from the rest. This Thanksgiving, I asked my mother why this seemingly inexpensive piece found a place among the other jewels.

She told me that when I was a tiny baby, we lived in a very small town in a very old house. In that old house, the crystal and china was on the top shelf as well, only the shelves weren't stable. One day a large truck rumbled down our street and shook our house. The top shelf of crystal shattered to the ground, breaking all but a few items.

My mother told me that was the one and only time she has ever cried over a possession. It was also the first time her children saw her cry. Unbeknownst to her, all six older children collected their nickels and dimes, walked together to the local variety store, and bought her the cut-glass dish. Now that simple little dish means more to her than any other piece she owns.

—*Julie M. Castle, Eugene, Oregon*

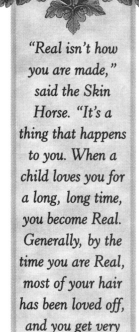

> "Real isn't how you are made," said the Skin Horse. "It's a thing that happens to you. When a child loves you for a long, long time, you become Real. Generally, by the time you are Real, most of your hair has been loved off, and you get very shabby."
>
> —MARGERY WILLIAMS, THE VELVETEEN RABBIT

With a little careful thought, you will be able to find a place where your most time-beloved possessions will feel safe and yet be nestled close to you. If you are nervous about damage, there's nothing wrong with investing in a glass-covered cabinet, a shadowbox, or a high, sturdy set of shelves. Treat your beloved possessions as you would any beloved friend—keep them comfortable, give them a break from time to time, pick them up, use them if possible.

Of course, this doesn't mean that the treasures you live with will be immune to the ravages of aging any more than you are. Chances are, your timeless treasures will suffer the occasional chip, scratch, or tear.

Despite your best care, your treasured crocheted tablecloth develops a brown stain.

Despite all his precautions, the two-year-old trips and breaks a teacup.

Your friend polishes the silverplated vase a bit too hard and exposes a copper strip.

And that hurts if you prize your treasure. But it will be all right if you remember why you loved it in the first place.

If your timeless treasure tells a story, each little crack and chip and worn spot becomes part of the ongoing tale. That stain recalls your fortieth anniversary party. The mended spot in the teacup reminds you of a treasured time of talk with a child now grown. The rosy stripe on the side of the vase reminds you of a friend who cared enough to help.

Those signs of aging are evidence of contact with real people and real lives. In place of that flawless, factory-bright finish, your timeless treasure will have the sheen of love and grace and character.

And, like a human being, your treasure will be all the more beautiful for having lived a little.

Treasures Transformed

When my grandmother, who was also my best friend, died suddenly six years ago, I felt the greatest loss I had yet experienced. Although she is no longer with me, she left behind a carefully preserved remnant of family treasures. These keepsakes no longer remain stored away in boxes or tucked away in drawers but have been transformed from old lace pillowcases into lovely antique curtains, from hand-stitched kitchen towels into decorative bed pillows, from torn antique quilts into little-girl vests and floppy hats as well as quilted stuffed bears and Christmas stockings.

These little treasures mean a lot to me. Grandma was always eager to tell the story about them to anyone who cared to listen. Now they are proudly displayed in my home.

I helped her frame one of them just before she died. It now hangs in my hallway. It is a handmade lace collar that belonged to my great-great-great grandmother. She wore this collar while traveling on a ship to the United States from France. She was indentured once she arrived to pay for her trip. It was during this trip on the boat that she met her husband, my great-great-great grandfather, who was also indentured. Once they arrived to the U.S., he worked out his term, then helped work out hers. They were then married. What a great love story!

—Sandra McCombs, Mounds, Oklahoma

Storing Treasures Safely

Treasures do best when they live close to you, but you can't have everything on your walls or your bedside table. Unfortunately, storage is where many of your treasures can be damaged because you can't see what is happening to them. Here are a few precautions to help you store your treasures safely.

• *Most treasures are happiest in the same climate and circumstances humans find comfortable.* They like a mild range of temperatures (65°-75°) and a moderate humidity (around 50 percent). This means that the wooden spoon your father carved your mother is better off hanging in your kitchen or your den than stored in your garage.

• *Protect your treasures from wood and ordinary paper.* Over time, the acid in wood and paper will stain and deteriorate cloth, paper, and photographs. Cover any wooden or paper surface your treasure might touch with acid-free paper (call your local museum to ask for sources) or muslin. Change paper or launder muslin every six months or so. You can also spray the inside of boxes or trunks with polyurethane spray or line them with aluminum foil.

• *Never store your treasures in plastic.* Dry-cleaning bags contain polyvinylchloride (PVC), which releases fiber-eating gases. Even "safe" plastic bags will trap moisture and increase the risk of mildew.

• *Avoid those "magnetic" photo albums* and any storage medium containing PVC, which do the same thing to your photos that it does to your clothes. Look for archival-quality photo pages made of polypropylene or mylar. Scrapbooks and journals made from acid-free paper will keep your treasures safe much longer.

• *Unframed prints and other pieces of artwork can be stored flat,* with pieces of acid-free paper in between, or carefully rolled inside a cardboard tube bigger than three inches across.

• *Use mats or spacers in frames* to keep the glass from touching fabric, photos, or prints. Ask a reputable frame shop for help in framing your treasures.

• *Clean any fabric item you plan to store* and rinse in distilled water to remove all traces of starch or chlorine bleach. Stains and starch in clothing tend to attract insects. Stains tend to set indelibly; bleach breaks down fibers.

• *Creasing can cut natural fibers, especially linen.* If possible, roll tablecloths or quilts on poles or tubes covered with muslin. If you must fold, fold loosely and tuck rolls of acid-free paper in the creases. Refold frequently in different patterns.

• *Beware of sun damage.* Ultraviolet light from the sun is a distinct danger to many objects. It can break down fibers as well as fade beautiful colors. (Fluorescent lights can be a source of fading as well.) Regularly rotate any treasures exposed to the sun. Instead of leaving one favorite print or painting on the wall by the window, let several pictures take turns. And why not choose an interior wall for your big arrangement of family photos?

• *Store silver away from any form of rubber.* Never tie bundles of silver flatware with a rubber band. If possible, store your silver with specially treated paper available in cooking-supply and department stores.

• *Pewter should not be housed in unpainted oak.* The tannin in the wood can damage the metal.

> *I have to come back to this place, this dear corner. Like the birds, I can both soar and nest. Unlike them, I can both dream and dust—often, at the same time.*
>
> —ELIZABETH CODY NEUWENHUYSE

What You Can Do with a Hankie

A hankie's a wonderful example of a timeless treasure that's beautiful, plentiful, and lends itself to many uses. In fact, about the only thing you're not likely to do with a really beautiful hankie these days is blow your nose. Here are some ideas.

- Use a hankie as a napkin on a tea tray.
- Lay flat, fill with potpourri, and gather with a ribbon for a quick sachet.
- Cut into hearts (with embroidered or lace corners) and applique onto a quilt.
- Use as the center for a decorative wall quilt.
- Drape over a small lampshade. (This can be a lovely use of a pretty pink hankie.)
- Gather several in a basket in the bathroom for use as fingertip towels.
- Give antique embroidered hankies as wedding gifts or party favors. Or embroider your own with the monograms of your friends.
- Use a colorful child's hankie from the fifties to sew a cute vest for your daughter's teddy bear.
- Tuck a lacy hankie into a suit pocket and let the lace peek out.
- Large hankies make pretty doilies for small tables. Try placing them under a lamp or a group of candles.metal.

Just the Right One

Times got hard when I became a young widow with four daughters and all the different roles I had to play. Once after a hard day's work, I was hurriedly trying to finish up my Christmas shopping, I was specifically looking for a doll for my youngest daughter. Though things were quite picked over and my budget tight, this one doll stood out with her bright-red Buster-Brown haircut and blue eyes. She was more expensive than I had planned for but I just knew she was the right doll. From the moment my daughter laid eyes on her Christmas morning she never left her side. Through the years her place on the bed was never empty, even though "Mildred," as she was affectionately called, was losing her hair and had mended arms and legs. She remained greatly loved. When my older daughter had her daughter, she fell in love with Mildred when she was two, and one day she just wouldn't let her go. Again Mildred fulfilled a little girl's childhood. My granddaughter had a daughter and passed Mildred on to her. Since then my youngest daughter is about to have her first child and is expecting a little girl. She is anxiously awaiting Mildred to come home. The sacrifice I made so many years ago has brought so much happiness and love, I don't regret a moment.

—Elaine Van Fleet, Placentia, California

Covered in Love

My treasure is a leather Bible cover that my mom gave me when I left home to go on the mission field. She had purchased it in the late 1960s or early 1970s. It is a wonderful token of her love for the Lord and her family. It is well worn from years of use.

—Eric P. Beatty, Eugene, Oregon

Love isn't love till you give it away.

—OSCAR HAMMERSTEIN

A Treasured Gift

A SHARING OF HEARTS AND HANDS

DON'T YOU JUST LOVE OPENING PRESENTS?

I do.

There's something about a gaily wrapped package that brings out the little girl in me.

I love the mystery. What can it be? Does is squish? Does it rattle?

I tingle at the suspense. I can't wait to see. And I thrill at the moment when the tissue is pulled aside and the treasure is finally revealed. Oh, look! . . .

What is there about gift giving (and receiving) that brings such fun and satisfaction? I think it's that giving helps us tap into the flowing current of loving relationships. It's a process that loosens our tight grip on "mine" and lets us reach out in openhanded wonder to touch each other, truly sharing our hearts and hands. No wonder it brings so much joy.

A true gift is an offering of the self. True gifts always come with a heart attached. Along with the treasure comes a little part of the giver as well.

At the simplest level, offering myself with a gift may just mean sharing my taste—giving the gift of what I like. Because I enjoy pretty, feminine objects, for instance, I am likely to give you something dainty or delicate. Because spiritual matters are important to me, my gift may have a spiritual focus. And because I enjoy digging around in flea markets and antique shops, there's always a strong likelihood that a gift from me will be an adopted treasure.

I keep a gift drawer in my breezeway full of special little items that have caught my eye. Whenever I go treasure hunting, I try to pick up a few special items for the drawer: a dainty little

dessert plate from an antique store, a set of embroidered linens from a rummage sale, a silver spoon from a flea market. Then, when a birthday or an anniversary or Christmas comes up, I go shopping first in my gift drawer.

Quite often I will hold on to a special gift for some time until I find the perfect recipient or until the right time comes to give the gift.

I once found two matched teacups in an antique store. They were very old and very delicate, obviously well loved. I bought them both with the idea that someday I would give one to a kindred spirit, someone who understands why the twin cups are special. Finally I gave my "kindred spirit" gift to the editor who helped me put together my teacup book. She tells me that whenever she drinks tea from that special cup, she thinks of me . . . and of course I think of her, too. The gift of kindred spirits has been a way for us to connect over many miles.

I'm thrilled that my friend liked her cup. But of course there was no guarantee that she would like it just because I liked it. So in addition to including a bit of myself in the gift, I had to take her own taste into account.

I loved the scene in the movie *The Joy Luck Club* when the mother names all the kind and unselfish things she has seen her grown daughter do. "I *see you*," the mother insists to the girl, who has felt inadequate and unappreciated. "I *see* you."

The Dress That Waited

Every time I see the white organdy baby dress in my grandmother's old trunk, I am reminded of a dream deferred and a dream come true. My mind goes back to 1966, when my husband and I, parents of two school-age boys, were expecting another baby. Of course, I was hoping for a girl. So I decided to transform my waltz-length wedding gown into a dainty baby dress. I spent hours tracing and cutting the intricate pattern. The tiny sleeves were hand sewn, the embroidered lace skirt scalloped just so. I laid the finished dress in the trunk. Several months later we were surprised with the birth of twin boys.

The dress stayed in the trunk. Although I relished those busy years in a household of four boisterous sons, I never forgot my longing for a little girl. I often opened the old trunk and touched the folds of organdy and lace, remembering that long-ago desire.

Years passed and our sons grew up and married. Then one day it happened. The scalloped organdy dress billowed over tiny satin slippers. Sunlight from stained-glass windows glanced off the silk bow in curly blond hair, and I smiled at the baby granddaughter nestled in my son's arms. My dream of a baby girl was finally a reality.

Since then the organdy dress from my wedding gown has become a priceless family heirloom, worn by other baby granddaughters on special family occasions. I like to think that the tradition will continue for many more years.

—Carolyn Camoriano, Kansas City, Missouri

And I believe the best gifts are given with that kind of open-eyed attention. We observe the people we are gifting—their dreams as well as their needs. We give thought and attention to choosing a gift that will speak to both, a gift that will be a treasure to them because it hits close to their heart.

I have always admired my friend Ellen for the thoughtfulness she puts into the gifts she gives. She takes her time and considers what the recipient is like, what would make him or her smile. She often comes up with creative ideas—like planting cactus on the patio for her desert-loving husband. Ellen's gifts are uniquely suited to their recipients, and they are usually treasured by those lucky people.

My Bob, too, likes to put that special element of thought into his gifts for me—and this can be a challenge because, at this point of my life, I already have so much! But one of my best-loved treasures is a tiny spoon he bought me for Mother's Day a few years back. A silver rose graces the handle, and the word *Mother* is inscribed in graceful script.

Now, Bob has bought me many more expensive gifts in our life together. Once for a birthday he gave me a very beautiful, very costly watch. It is absolutely perfect for me; I will never need another watch in my life. But you know, as much as I love my watch . . . I really treasure that little spoon. I love the thoughtfulness of that gift. I love the fact that Bob took time to consider what I really like, what moves me and makes me happy, and that he spent precious hours combing through antique stores to find it.

When it comes to giving a treasure, it truly is the thought that counts—the sentiment, the intent, especially "seeing" the other person. And time is also important, for treasured gifts almost always involve an investment of time.

It takes time to think carefully about just the right gift for someone. It takes time to visit one more shop, read through one more catalog. It takes time to create a handmade treasure or even to wrap a gift in pretty paper and tie it with a ribbon.

And time, of course, can be a gift in itself. Some of the most treasured memories result from gifts of time and shared experience.

An Angel Every Year

As I was growing up, my family opened Christmas presents very carefully so as not to tear the paper. The paper and name tags were saved and used the next year, and the next year, and so on.

I am not sure when the angel tag first appeared, but the first present I remember it being on was a portable typewriter when I was in high school. (I think it was a secondhand typewriter, but that didn't matter to me.) The tag was a folded 2 x 2 inch card with the picture of an angel on the outside and my name written on the inside. The next year the same tag appeared again on my Christmas gift, and after I left home, it arrived on the Christmas gift my parents sent me in the mail.

For fun I sent the tag back to my mother, and it returned at Christmas . . . again and again. The gift was nearly always something my mother had made—clothes or that great Christmas candy she always made right after Thanksgiving. I continued to send the tag right back.

I am not sure just when, but at some point I realized that my mother was no longer able to make or buy something for us and get it mailed. So one year, I kept the tag for good. One of the last gifts I received with this tag was a blue-checked apron, which I usually pull out at Christmas. This doesn't match the Christmas decorations and food, but I think it very appropriate.

Mother is now ninety-four years old and in a nursing home. I still hold on to my angel gift tag, with its memories of many Christmases past and of her love for me.

—Betty Purvis Christian, Waco, Texas

A meal cooked and beautifully served is a gift of time. So is a caring conversation and attentive listening. A driving lesson, a shared walk in the park, a Monopoly game—all these are loving donations of the most precious gift any of us have to give: a portion of the finite number of hours we have to spend on this earth.

Family traditions are, in essence, the ongoing gift of time and togetherness we give each other. When we nurture our traditions and carry them on, we give each other the precious gifts of continuity and security and identity.

In case you haven't noticed, children are fierce guardians of traditions. They protect family rituals with the same care they guard their little boxes full of owl feathers and pretty rocks. This is because children understand rituals are keys to comfort and security. Traditions say, "You are part of us because we've always done this, and now you're doing it too."

When I asked my own grown children about their timeless treasures and treasured memories, their first thoughts were of family traditions. Jenny remembered that we always went out for burgers on Saturday nights. Both children remember that Bob always read the Christmas story on Christmas morning before we trooped in to see what Santa had brought. That family ritual is the cornerstone of their happy Christmas memories, treasured more than any gift that was under the tree.

And yet children aren't the only ones who benefit from the gift of tradition. Adults thrive on traditions because they connect us with our past and our future. Traditions are a reminder that even in a quickly changing world, some things continue. That we will "do it again" and, in the process, we will continue to be close.

What more precious gift can we give the ones we love than the gift of memory and continuity? Carrying on a tradition is yet another gift of our precious time.

But time is not only a component of gift treasures or just a gift in itself. Time has the power to bring out the treasure in other gifts—to show us which gifts are truly treasures for us.

I'm so glad now that I held onto some of the things my auntie passed on to me before she died. This auntie had always been generous with me, and in the years before her death she gave me many of her treasures to take home. Most of these I stored away because they just weren't me. But later, after my aunt's death, I started to feel differently about her treasures. They reminded me of her, and I found I wanted them around me. One by one, they have emerged from storage to take their place beside my other treasures.

My daughter-in-law Maria, who is wise beyond her years, understands this treasure principle. That is why she holds onto a vase and small green bowl that belonged to her grandmother. These fussy, old-fashioned pieces are definitely not a fit in Maria's simple, unfussy household. And yet when husband Brad set them out to be sold at their garage sale, Maria quickly swept them back inside. Now they hide in the back of her china cabinet, patiently waiting. Someday, I suspect, Maria will have them on proud display. She will find a way to keep them as part of her life.

Time has an amazing power to bring out the love and meaning in a gift-treasure. The love and meaning can gradually transform the objects themselves in our eyes. Even if a gift is not "you," you may grow to love it. Even if it isn't beautiful, it may someday be beautiful to you because it says "somebody loved me."

And that, of course, is the message of all true gifts. They say you are worth my time and my thought and my consideration. In at least a small sense, you are worth giving up something of myself in order to connect with you.

> *It is possible to give without loving, but it is impossible to love without giving.*
>
> —RICHARD BRAUNSTEIN

The Star and the Heart

When my dreamy, precious granddaughter Kelsey Lee was two years old, sitting between her mommy and daddy at my surprise sixtieth birthday party dinner, I walked by and patted her on her golden curls and whispered in her ear, "You're my star." She turned around, looked at me with those laughing, loving eyes and replied, "Grammy, you my heart." Since that night, whenever we talk on the phone or send cards and letters, she's been my star and I'm her heart! She will always draw a heart by my name and draw a star by her name. I will always smile at this most treasured tradition.

—*Shirley Hawkins, Eugene, Oregon*

There are even times when I may choose to give up one of my own treasures to say *I love you* to someone who is special in my life. I may choose to pass along not something from my gift drawer, not something I have carefully selected in a shop, but something from my home. Something that has come to have special significance to me.

But I have to admit, that kind of giving is not easy for me.

The truth is that I love my things. They bring me comfort. I love to keep them around me. And part of me just knows nobody else can love them and care for a timeless treasure the way I can.

Oh yes, I love to share. I like to play show-and-tell with my special possessions. And I love to shop for people and give them gifts.

But sometimes, when I'm preparing to give away something really special, something I've worked hard to find, something really different I've uncovered in a shop, something I just know they're going to love because I love it so . . . well, I feel a little tug. That impossibly delicate little porcelain clock would look so perfect over there by the window. . . .

Other times, I feel that little nudge inside that says it's time to pass something on. It's time to give Grandma's teacup to Jenny, to take out my daddy's ring and give it to Chad.

And yet . . . and yet I'm not ready.

You probably have moments when you feel the same way. And there's nothing really wrong with that. After all, your treasures wouldn't be treasures unless you loved or valued them. They are your touchstones; they remind you of who you are. Giving them away feels like parting with an old friend.

The Bottomless Gift of Love

When I went home this Christmas, I knew my father had only a short while to live. I realized that whatever gift I chose would be the last I would ever give to him. More than anything, I wanted to give him something I had made myself. Because I didn't know if I would be at home when he died, I wanted it to be something that would remind him of my love every day. . . . So I took an old paprika can, painted it red, and wrote "love" on both sides. My mom and sister sprinkled it liberally on Dad every day until he passed away. And just like love, it never ran out.

—Betty Fletcher, Eugene, Oregon

Keeping the Pieces Together

My grandfather and I used to put puzzles together. It was a great way to be with him while he had cancer. After he died, I received the last puzzle we ever put together. It is now once more together and framed up in my bedroom. It reminds me of him and all the special talks we had while putting the puzzles together.

—Lea Ann Myers, Placentia, California

But this I am learning, sometimes reluctantly, about treasures: In order for our story to have its richest telling, our treasures their deepest meaning, we need to be willing to give them away.

There's a difference between enjoying our treasures and clasping them too tightly in our hot little hearts. It's the difference that determines whether love continues to flow freely in our lives. It's the difference, I think, that makes our treasures timeless. For in the end, it's the treasures we give away that will be most surely ours.

It has been nearly ten years ago now since I lost fourteen of my favorite teacups. A glass shelf shifted, and before I knew it those cups shattered on the floor. I told myself they were just teacups, but a little part of my heart shattered along with them. Some were family heirlooms, others represented treasured memories. I mourned the loss of these old friends.

And then I went away to speak at a seminar. My hostess for the weekend welcomed me warmly and showed me around her lovely house. This was a woman who obviously enjoyed her treasures and cared for them lovingly. I especially admired a beautiful set of dishes in her china cabinet. She had a complete setting for twelve, with beautiful dainty pink roses scattered on creamy porcelain.

"They *are* special," she agreed when I exclaimed over them. "I've always been proud of them. I wish the pattern hadn't been discontinued."

Then we went in to dinner. We talked. We got to know each other. Gradually, we became friends. With some sadness, I shared my story about the shattered teacups.

My bounty is as boundless as the sea, My love as deep; the more I give to thee, The more I have, for both are infinite.

—WILLIAM SHAKESPEARE

The next morning at breakfast, I found a pink-sprigged teacup filled with steaming tea next to my plate. Tears filled my eyes at her thoughtfulness.

"I want to thank you for sharing your teacup with me this morning," I said. "It makes the morning special."

"Oh, it's your teacup now," she told me. "It's my gift to you. Maybe it'll help get your collection going again."

The tears still spring to my eyes when I think of that gift, which holds a place of honor in my china cabinet. Whenever I see it, I think of that beautiful woman and her now incomplete set of eleven teacups.

I have no way of knowing what difference her sacrifice has made in her life, whether she remembers it as vividly as I do.

But I know one thing.

Her gift is a timeless treasure that will always keep that special friend close to my heart.

She taught me how important it is to hold all my treasures with a light hand, caring for them with gratitude but being willing to hand them over joyfully when the time comes. When love commands.

It's a lesson worth remembering whenever we are contemplating our beautiful treasures because, after all, we can't take them with us. Eventually, we will leave behind our earthly treasures. And then we will be remembered not by what we've kept, but by what we've given away.

The flow of giving and receiving, of loving and sharing, is what will keep us connected to the stream of time and memory.

I will be remembered not for the bottle of perfume I hoarded away, but for the silver teapot I found for Maria's birthday. Not for the quilts I have stacked in a corner, but the quilt I tucked up around a child's neck prior to a bedtime story. Not for the teacups placed high in a cabinet, but for the teacup that held a shared cup of tea and a prayer—or the teacup I gave away.

This is a lesson most of us have to keep relearning, but it's the truth that will set us free: I only get to keep what I give away.

And that understanding, more precious than any diamond, is the gift I want to pass on to the ones I love.

The Gift of a Memory

The very best gifts are the gifts of your time that come with a memory attached. It's easy to give this treasure to the people you love!

Write a letter on a special occasion and save it to give to the recipient later. One mother I know wrote a letter to her newborn, expressing all her hopes and dreams and prayers for the little girl's future. She plans to "mail" that letter on her daughter's eighteenth birthday.

Have family photographs copied at your local camera shop and give the copies as gifts. Frame the photos, put them in albums, or make a collage. Be sure and attach an explanation of who, what, when, and where!

Take children on a "memory journey" to visit places that were important to you as a child: the house where you were born, the town where you went to college, the building where you had your first job.

Nurture a family tradition—or start a new one. Enjoy special traditions with your friends as well: a reunion breakfast once a year, a progressive dinner at Christmastime, a summer camping trip.

Plan a special ceremony to pass along an heirloom to a child or a friend.

Teach a skill that was passed along to you by someone you loved: carving, crocheting, or skipping stones across a pond.

Videotape a family gathering or special event and distribute copies.

Research your family tree and make copies for others in your family. If you are handy with a needle, why not put it on a felt banner or a needlepoint pillow?

Tell the stories! Grab every opportunity, especially while your children are small, to pass along the family stories you've heard and to tell your own story. This is the first and best way to pass on the gift of your family heritage.

New Gifts from Old

Some of the most creative and meaningful gifts involve old treasures. Some are handmade from bits and pieces; others are carefully sought and chosen. Either way, chances are your gift will be unique and appreciated.

• Frame a montage of childhood keepsakes—baby rings, christening gowns, hospital bracelets, even a lock of hair—and give it to a grown child as a keepsake.

• Go gift shopping in your local antique store or flea market. A dainty dessert plate, a spoon, a pair of antique booties—so many adopted items make delightful wedding or birthday gifts.

• Use pieces of broken china pottery to make unique gifts. Piece together with grout to make a mosaic tray or box lid. Or add hardware to make earrings or pins. If edges are sharp, sand with fine sandpaper dipped in oil.

• Have an old ring reset with a new stone or a beautiful old jewel enhanced by a new setting—and give it to your teenager.

• Antique buttons can be used in collages or to decorate clothing. My friend Lisa made a stunning holiday vest with a Christmas tree on it and used her button collection for the ornaments.

• Save satin and lace left over from making (or altering) a wedding dress to cover a wedding album, make a pillow or a ring pillow, trim a baby dress.

• Surprise a friend with a gift of vintage clothing—a hat, a camisole, or even a dress. Or try decorating a hat or a men's suit vest with antique lace and pieces of costume jewelry.

Take it—'tis a gift of love— that seeks thy good alone; Keep it for the giver's sake, and read it for thine own.

YOUTH'S KEEPSAKE, 1836

Lost and Found Treasure

Secret trips to the basement. Pounding and sawing sounds caught the attention of my sister Elain and me. We were living in Milwaukee when we were four and five years old. It was during the Depression, and no money was available for Christmas gifts.

At Christmas we were presented a beautiful two-story dollhouse with electric lights, a fireplace, a staircase and window boxes. It was beautifully painted inside and out by our father. There were curtains for the windows, rugs for the floors, and beautiful furniture made by our mother. We loved that dollhouse and played with it for many years.

As teenagers we put it in the basement of the church in a small Wisconsin town where my father was the pastor. The children played with it during children's church and when they were fussy in church and the mothers had to take them out of the service.

Eventually it was forgotten as the years went by until my husband and I took our children on a trip from California to the places I lived growing up in Wisconsin. When we went to the little church, to my surprise, there was the dollhouse we left there many years before. The kind pastor allowed us to take it home with us. A lost treasure was found—a wonderful remembrance of a loving mother and father.

—Mary Ellen Congelliere Huhn
Santa Ana, California

*For where your treasure is,
there will your heart be also.*

—THE GOSPEL OF MATTHEW

The Gift of Every Day

AN EPILOGUE

In the end, of course, they're all just things.

I love my teacups, love my quilts, love my photos and my letters and my albums . . . but they are still just things, and things are not what matters in the long run.

What does matter, of course, is people. What matters is relationships. What matters is love and memory.

And if I ever forget that, if I ever let my material treasures get in the way of what really matters, I will have missed the whole point—and lost my truest treasure.

Very little that I own will stand the test of the centuries.

Most of my possessions will eventually be lost or rusted or cracked or crumbled or picked up by somebody in an antique shop who never knew my name.

But the time I invest today in my family, in my friends, in those I love, will never be wasted or lost. For the time and energy I invest in loving others has truly timeless potential. It has the capacity to shape memories, to shape souls. And it is this that gives my legacy its meaning.

It is the tea parties I have now with my grandchildren that will make their inherited teacups precious to them.

It is the love I give them now that will make them want to keep my photo on the wall.

It is the stories I tell them today that will make them want to pass my stories on to their own children.

It is what I do today that determines what becomes of my life and my name tomorrow.

Every day, then, is a timeless treasure.

It is far more beautiful, far more valuable, than the most priceless material heirloom because it gives me the opportunity to invest in the hearts and souls of the people I love.

And that's true for you, too.

This day is the greatest treasure you own.

So hold it close.

Inhale its fragrance.

Learn its lessons.

And then let it go, to become a treasured memory as you walk forward step by step into eternity.